Conversations
That Make a Difference

Shift Your Beliefs to Get What You Want

Wake Up Women

In collaboration with

Burge Smith-Lyons and Essence of Being

Parker House Publishing
www.ParkerHouseBooks.com

© 2014 Wake Up Women LLC

All rights reserved.

This material in this book is intended for entertainment. No legal, medical or other professional advice is implied or expressed. No part of this book may be used in any manner whatsoever without written permission from Wake Up Women LLC. P.O. Box 774, Mayflower, Arkansas 72016
501-232-1175

Foreword

Debbie Allen

As an entrepreneur, my background in business started at a very young age, but I had no formal business training except for learning from the school of hard knocks. I built and sold numerous million dollar companies and although I've had many successes in my life, one day I felt something was missing. That "something" was giving back to others. I had been blessed with many wonderful mentors in my life and believed it was time for me to begin supporting and mentoring others in return. At the time I had no idea that I was going to become a business expert; actually, I didn't even know how to go about it.

It's the shift in belief from "How can I make money?" to "What can I do to serve others?" that has made a difference in my life. When you let go of just chasing the next dollar and focus on how to best share your gifts and talents with the world you begin to develop a business around your passion and, when done well, money and opportunities begin to flow easily and consistently to you.

You've heard the saying, "Do what you love, and the money will follow."

Is this actually true? If you follow your passion and pursue what you love doing for a living, will the monetary rewards really follow? What I've discovered is that it certainly helps - but you'll need more than that to grow a lucrative career that supports others in return. Having passion will give you the drive and determination you'll need when the road gets rocky or times get challenging. Skills and talent are required to make a name for yourself; but passion, skills and talent alone won't pay the bills.

We all have a life journey, a story, a message, or skills that will help and inspire others. What matters most is how we share our message. You were born into this world to make a difference by giving back to others in some way. When you share your gifts with the world, you begin to receive the most amazing gifts in return with a more fulfilled and enriched life.

You'll know when this commitment of giving back feels right because you will truly be living and breathing your own legacy … Yes, LIVING your legacy … not just leaving it behind when you exit the planet.

If you have ever been mentored, guided or coached by someone in any way, you understand the feeling of being supported by someone who believes in you. Maybe they even believed in you more than you believed in yourself at that time. This may have caused a shift in you, too. Your beliefs where shifted and changed forever making you a better person in some way.

A shift, no matter how small, can be a life-changing experience.

When you've been supported, it makes you want to support others in having the same type of shift. Imagine a life of giving back by lifting others up in the form of inspiration, motivation, knowledge and the commitment to do better; shifting them to a better life in some way. Imagine being able to support others in this same magical way while passing on your own experiences.

Every positive shift in someone's life holds energy. This same energy continues to grow and consistently expands. When you help others do better and believe in themselves, everyone around them does better, too.

The best way to give to others is not with presents - but with your presence. That's truly your gift!

What gifts of presence will you share with the world? Your special gifts and talents are priceless. They come in the form of your skills, passion, vision, wisdom, enthusiasm and commitment.

Everyone has gifts to share and you also have an 'expert' just waiting inside to get out and step up to a bigger game. When you step up, the world will take notice and be there waiting to hear your words.

Stepping up to a bigger game in business and in life means stepping up to 'owning' your passion by become the expert at what you know and love as you support others with your wisdom and experiences.

I invite you to read and experience the shift in beliefs that are openly shared by the authors whose stories make a difference in the pages that follow.

Learn more about stepping up to a bigger game by joining Debbie Allen's Expert Community at
www.TheHighlyPaidExpert.com.

Much success and happiness,
Debbie Allen,
The Expert of Experts

About the author

Debbie Allen, The Expert of Experts has been ranked as one of the top 3% of professional women speakers worldwide. She has been a professional business speaker for the past 20 years and has presented before thousands of people in 28 countries around the world.

Debbie is an award-winning entrepreneur and bestselling author of six books including her newest book *The Highly Paid Expert*. She has built and sold six million dollar companies in diverse industries. Today, she supports clients in developing brand domination around their expertise. Debbie works with small business owners, entrepreneurs, coaches, speakers and experts of all kinds. Learn more and sign up for her training programs at www.DebbieAllen.com.

Introduction

The Day Before...The Day After

Karen Mayfield

Habits... we all have them. Every living breathing thing on the planet, every day, will go about their days unconsciously operating out of habit. Animals, for the purpose of survival, repeat processes without thinking. As humans, we wake up each morning, get our favorite beverage, prepare for our day, and most of the time, our today is a lot like our yesterday, which often leads to our tomorrow being just like our yesterday and today. Happy, sad or somewhere in between, we just continue with our usual way of doing things.

Then it happens! Something comes along to instantly change our way of going about our day. A tragedy strikes; maybe we lose our job, a loved one passes away, natural disasters hit, and instantly our habits and our usual way of doing things immediately changes. We start living in the moment, taking each step differently than the step before.

Recently, I had a chance to not just encounter change; I also had the opportunity to witness human behavior in a form that altered my thoughts and beliefs. A devastating tornado ravaged our small town, as well as a neighboring town, leaving thousands of people homeless, injured, and some even lost their lives. Millions of dollars in damage occurred. In the blink of an eye, *everything* had changed. In less than five minutes the storm altered people's lives forever. What happened next was humanity at its best.

Within minutes of the storm passing, people were checking on every one to make sure they were okay. My phone was ringing constantly with people checking on me, the farm and all the animals. One of my friends even drove through downed trees on debris covered roads in his truck to get to me and make sure everything was okay. Others were digging people out from under rubble, stepping up to help mankind without giving any thought to how much they were going to get paid. It was not about the money, money was the last thing on the minds of those people that day; they were there to help any way they could.

The day after the storm there were thousands of volunteers who came to help their fellow Americans. They came with chainsaws, tree trimmers, heavy equipment and whatever was needed and available to help. The help came from our local citizens and others from around the country showing up at their own expense to lend a helping hand. Search and Rescue pages for missing animals were established on social media, pages for people needing help were created. People who still had their homes were opening their doors to those homes giving strangers a place to rest and regroup.

The local restaurant in our town became the place where we would gather over the next week for a good meal and fellowship with other citizens to see how we could help each other. Whatever we needed, there was someone at the restaurant that knew where we could get it.

We went for days without power or water, and two-thirds of our infrastructure for commerce was completely blown away. Volunteers were coordinated and quickly assembled, injured animals were being treated free of charge. Within days FEMA and the Red Cross were mobilized and on site, ready to help. The local news shared stories of heroism amid the devastation. Volunteers shared their stories of what it was like to help in the process of picking up pieces of someone's life from a picture frame with a family photo, a child's toy and numerous keepsakes. Radio stations were interviewing victims, and sharing stories of people who had been through the storm. These broadcasts shared with the world how the tragedy that happened in less than five minutes changed the lives of thousands, and at the same time, brought out the best in thousands of others. Even with help from many from seemingly everywhere, it will take a long time to get our town back to where it was before the storm.

Tragedy strikes every day. More and more natural disasters are occurring; just watch the news and you will see firsthand accounts of lives being altered in one way or another. Shocking as it may be and as hard as it is to believe, none of us are exempt. Tragedy can strike any one of us at any time without warning or preparation.

Reflecting back to 9-11-2001 when the USA was hit with a manmade tragedy, we watched in horror as an act that seemed so surreal it must be made for TV entertainment unfolded before our very eyes. From that tragedy the humanism and humanitarianism that was forthcoming was unending. For the first time I saw Americans standing united as a nation, not separated by a political party. Hurricane Katrina in 2005 and hurricane Sandy in 2012 proved, yet again, that in a crisis, humans will unite to help each other.

Wild fires, floods, random shootings, whatever the tragedy, out from the rubble and the blood comes the humanism that exists in each of us.

But why does it take a tragedy to bring out one of the best GOD given qualities a human possesses; our ability to give freely, our happy to help attitude, and our ability to reach out and touch each other in ways that are not politically driven, money motivated, or race and religiously separated. *The Knowledge Book* teaches that *"we who live on the face of the planet live under the roof of the world as a whole, a family."* So why does it take a tragedy to bring the human family together?!

We know tragedy is going to happen, and humanity will do what we do, but I would like to propose an idea. I invite you to stop for a moment and think about your life and how unconscious your goal is to just GO ON AND LIVE, get through the day, make it another week, day or month. Are we so consumed with surviving that we block our own thriving?

What if each person reading these words would make a commitment to take time from our busy schedules and consciously reach out and touch someone with help, don't make it about the money, don't worry about the color of the other person's skin, their religion or political party. Instead, reach out to help your family member and do that for and with three people each day. Did you know that within 19 days nearly everybody on the planet would be reaching out to help someone? Talk about a wave of gratitude! Imagine the vibrational impact that could easily alter the happenings on the planet. We can and will create a world where Peace of Mind as a state of mind is the missing Peace to the puzzle. The question is: Will you accept the challenge?

In the words of Napoleon Hill from his book *Grow Rich with Peace of Mind*, I want to share with you these thoughts:

> *"In addition to money-success, we seek Peace of Mind to make our lives complete. A life free from worries, unhappiness, self-induced illness, nervous tension, fear, is possible and it all starts not with a hand out but a hand up. When we speak of Peace of Mind we speak of more than peace as a restful state. Peace of Mind is called the wealth without which you cannot really be wealthy."*

If hurt people hurt people then how can we heal the hurt to stop the hurt? The day before tragedy is like most other days, the day after the tragedy, regardless of your financial situation, or your belief or your political affiliation is unlike any other day you have already experienced. What you will need is not the governmental help that is available, it will take a while for that to trickle down to you; what you truly need is the *Human Resource*, because that is the only resource there really is.

The stories you are about to read are stories of courage, in which you will find what you need.

About the author

Karen Mayfield is the founder of Wake up Women, Author, Speaker, Metaphysical Minister, and Spiritual Life Coach.

Join Karen as she takes you into the world and brand of Wake up Women while guiding you through your process of waking up to your life of happiness, health & wealth, with Peace of mind to live the life you love. To learn more about Karen visit www.wakeupwomen.com

Preface

Using Your Power to Create Success and Significance

Excerpt from
Think and Grow Rich for Women

Sharon Lechter

The rules of success are the same for everyone. Why mess with the brilliance of Napoleon Hill's original book, *Think and Grow Rich*? Why write something just for women?

These questions and many more, are sure to be asked. In fact, for most of my career, I have felt the same way. I originally read *Think and Grow Rich* when I was nineteen and have read it many times during my career and it has had a huge impact on my life.

My parents taught me that I could be anyone or do anything I wanted as long as I worked hard and focused on my goals. They had worked hard all their lives and were fabulous role models. It wasn't until I started my career, all alone in a different city, that reality started to set in. It was in the late 1970's and I was one of only a few women in my field, and so I quickly learned that I definitely had to work harder than my male counterparts if I wanted to get ahead. So I did.

No one said it would be easy — and it wasn't. No one said it would be a smooth ride — and it hasn't been. But the resilience and lessons learned from facing and surviving the rough times were essential contributors to my success today.

Now more than thirty-five years later, I continue to be amazed by the stories of the incredible businesswomen I meet and how they, too, in the face of the glass ceiling or sexual bias, found ways to forge ahead. Many of them had read and followed the teachings of *Think and Grow Rich* and created great success in their lives, but they have gone even further. They have each taken their success in stride and continued on to open new paths for the women who follow them, evolving their lives of success into lives of significance.

Think and Grow Rich for Women is a celebration of these women and every woman who has succeeded in spite of the obstacles they have encountered — women who have changed history, created great business success, and provided great opportunities for others.

In addition, there have been some incredible economic developments that have brought greater attention to successful women, and in doing so, have revealed that while the rules may be the same, women approach those rules differently, and they apply them differently than men do. While there is still much progress to be made, there has been a "quiet revolution" as women have gained momentum in every aspect of life. The following statistics showing the increasing power of women are the most recent available at the time of this writing.

In the Economy

The financial statistics prove, without a doubt, that women have tremendous power and influence globally. Can you imagine what would happen if women came together and utilized their economic power to create positive change?

- 60 percent of all personal wealth in the United States is held by women.

- 85 percent of all consumer purchases in the United States are made by women.

- Women over the age of fifty have a combined net worth of $19 trillion.

- Two-thirds of consumer wealth in the United States will belong to women in the next decade.

- $7 trillion is spent by women in the United States in consumer and business spending.

- Globally, women are responsible for $20 trillion in spending, and that number is expected to rise to $28 trillion by the end of 2014.

- Globally, women stand to inherent 70 percent of the $41 trillion in intergenerational wealth transfer expected over the next forty years.

In Education

The United States Department of Education estimated that for 2013 women earned:
- 61.6 percent of all associate degrees
- 56.7 percent of all bachelor's degrees

- 59.9 percent of all master's degrees
- 51.6 percent of all doctorate degrees

In summary, in 2013 140 women graduated with a college degree at some level for every hundred men.

In the Corporate World
While tremendous progress has been made in the lower ranks of management, there is still a great need for women to advance at the higher levels of leadership in corporations, which is evident that the glass ceiling still needs to be shattered:

- There are twenty four, or 4.8 percent, women CEO's of Fortune 500 companies.

- Women hold 14 percent of executive officer positions.

According to a report by Catalyst titled *The Bottom Line: Corporate Performance and Women's Representation on Boards,* Fortune 500 companies with the highest representation of women board directors attained significantly higher financial performance, on average, than those with the lowest representation of women board directors. In addition, the report highlights that boards with three or more women directors show notably stronger-than-average performance. It shared three key measurements:

1. Return on Equity: On average, companies with the highest percentage of women board directors out performed those with the least by 53 percent.

2. Return on Sales: On average, companies with the highest percentage of women board directors outperformed those with the least by 42 percent.

3. Return on Invested Capital: On average, companies with the highest percentage of women board directors outperformed those with the least by 66 percent. Women hold 16.6 percent of board seats in the United States, as compared to 40.9 percent in Norway, and 6 percent in Asia.

It is important to note that Norway passed a law in 2003 requiring companies to appoint women to 40 percent of board posts.

A study of companies in the MSCI AC World index, which is an index to measure the equity market performance of developed markets in twenty-four countries, found that companies with a gender diverse board outperformed those with only men by 26 percent over six years.

In Earnings

While the overall statistics are still disturbing, when you dig into the detail, a positive trend is emerging:

- Women are paid an average of $.77 for every dollar men make. IN 1970, it was $.59.

- While the $.77 statistic has remained constant over the last few years, a total of sixteen states report that their women are earning $.80 or more for every dollar men make.

- When you exclude self-employment and workers who only work part of the year, in 2012 women earned 80.9 percent as much as men.

And a review by age group shows significant improvement for younger women. According to the bureau of Labor Statistics:

Pay Equity by Age

Age Group	Women's Percentage of Men's Earnings
20-24	93.2 percent
25-34	92.3 Percent
35-44	78.5 Percent
45-54	76.0 Percent
55-64	75.1 Percent
65+	80.9 Percent

Globally, men's median, full time earnings were 17.6 percent higher than women's in developing countries. The biggest gender wage gap was in South Korea and Japan.

Globally, according to a Deloitte study, women's earning power is growing faster than men's in developing countries. Their earned incomes have increased by 8.1 percent compared with 5.8 percent for men.

In Business Ownership
More and more women are shunning the corporate world in favor of entrepreneurship, thereby circumventing the impact of the glass ceiling all together. The *State of Women-*

Owned Businesses Report for 2013 (commissioned by American Express OPEN) reveals:

- Between 1997 and 2013, the number of women-owned firms has grown at one and a half times the national average;

- The number of women-owned and equally owned firms is nearly 13.6 million and they:
Generate more than $2.7 trillion in revenues these firms employ nearly 15.9 million people; these firms represent 46 percent of U.S. firms and contribute 13 percent of total employment and 8 percent of firm revenues.

In Politics

More women are entering politics than ever before. The following statistics, however, show there is still a far way to go to reach parity with male political leaders.

Globally:
There are thirty female leaders in countries of self-ruling territories.

In the United States, women hold:
- 20 percent of seats in the U.S. Senate
- 17.9 percent of seats in the U.S. House of Representatives
- 23.1 percent of state-level elective offices.

As women realize their economic power, and start leveraging it, these statistics will continue to improve.

Women are making wonderful progress in each of these areas and it is time to celebrate, instead of complain! Let's change the dialogue about women from one of complain about how bad things are for women to one of celebration of our accomplishments. Just by shifting from a negative dialogue to a positive one, the underlying beliefs of women will begin to change as well.

Women will believe they can choose their own pathway to success.

Women will believe they can succeed in business, and be wonderful mothers and have a happy family life as well.

Women will change their belief of wanting to achieve balance in their lives and break the guilt cycle it brings and begin to realize that their natural talents and strengths are needed for the future of the economy.

When women believe in themselves, they will not only be successful… they will lead lives of significance.

Think and Grow Rich for Women
THE FUTURE IS YOUR CHOICE
Please visit www.sharonlechter.com/women to create your personalized blueprint.

We Want to Hear Your Story
Visit our global community online of women where you can share your inspiration, your challenges, your triumphs, and how you pursue your definite purpose each day. Whether you are just starting or well on your way to your One Big Life, there is a community of women waiting to

support you, be lifted up by you, and to guide you down the path of living a life of success and significance.

Order your copy today. www.sharonlechter.com/women

About the Author

Sharon Lechter is an entrepreneur, philanthropist, author, educator, international speaker, CPA, CGMA and mother. She is CEO of Pay Your Family First, an organization dedicated to financial education. Sharon is the co-author of the bestselling books *Rich Dad Poor Dad*, *Outwitting the Devil*, *Three Feet From Gold*, *Save Wisely, Spend Happily* and author of her newest book *Think and Grow Rich for Women*. Sharon served on the first President's Advisory Council on Financial Literacy, as a national spokesperson for the AICPA's Commission on Financial Literacy. The National Bank of Arizona recognized her as its 2013 Woman of the Year and she was honored by *AZ Business Magazine* as one of the 50 most Influential Women in Arizona Business. Sharon serves on the National Boards for Women's Presidents Organization, EmpowHer and *Enterprising Women Magazine*. Sharon lives each day in pursuit of, and to inspire others to achieve, a life of success and significance.

Connect with Sharon at: www.sharonlechter.com

Table of contents

FOREWORD III

    DEBBIE ALLEN VI

INTRODUCTION
THE DAY BEFORE...THE DAY AFTER VII

    KAREN MAYFIELD XII

PREFACE
USING YOUR POWER TO CREATE SUCCESS
AND SIGNIFICANCE XIII

    EXCERPT FROM THINK AND GROW RICH FOR WOMEN
    SHARON LECHTER XXII

THE STORIES

    BREAK DOWN, BREAK THROUGH, BREAK FREE! 1

        BURGE SMITH-LYONS 8

    BUILDING BELIEF 9

        RITA DAVENPORT 16

    TAKE BACK YOUR IDENTITY
    RECLAIM YOUR TRUE SELF TO BECOME YOUR BEST 17

        DIANNE REILLY 24

    COURAGE - THE DAY I FOUND IT
    MY JOURNEY TO ECKHART TOLLE 25

        MICHELE PENN 32

CLEARING THE CLUTTER TO CLARIFY YOUR MISSION™ 33

Alexandra Figueredo 41

CLAIM YOUR TRUTH 42

Linda Satya Tsai 50

ARMOR OF WISDOM 51

Deidre Trudeau 58

ARE YOU ONE OF THE LIVING DEAD? 59

Amani Jackson 64

THE SHIFT FROM GRIEF TO GRACE 65

Christine Gregory Campos 72

YOUR BEST YOU: *UNLEASHED!!!* 73

Deborah Respress 80

COOKING FOR PERSONAL TRANSFORMATION 81

Rachael J. Avery 89

THE ULTIMATE POWER OF CHANGING YOUR BELIEFS! 90

Dame DC Cordova 98

BE THE LIFE 99

Melodee Meyer 104

MIRACLES HAPPEN WHEN YOU LOVE YOURSELF 105

Dr. Annie Lim 111

BORN TO BE ALIVE - YOUR LIFE, YOUR MESSAGE 112

Jim T. Chong 119

IMPERFECTION TO PERFECTION: HOW I MANIFESTED MY PERFECT LOVING SOUL MATE 120

    Paula Hopwood 128

FROM CRAZED TO CLARITY AND COMPASSION 129

    Rosie Aiello 136

FROM LOSS TO LOVE 137

    MarBeth Dunn 143

LET'S TALK ABOUT
FROM DEATH DO US PART TO LIFE THAT WE LIVE 144

    Shawneen Rubay 151

SHIFT HAPPENS - BELIEVING IS SEEING 152

    Candi Parker 159

WHEN I "WALKED IN" TO MY LIFE EVERYTHING CHANGED 160

    Ariel Albani 167

HOW I LOST MY MIND AND FOUND MY HEART 168

    Don Milton 175

FROM PIECES TO PEACE THREE MINUTES AT A TIME 176

    Dina Proctor 183

THE GIFT OF GRATITUDE 184

    Teresa Velardi 190

THERE'S ANOTHER WAY OF LOOKING AT THIS
SEEING FROM A HIGHER PERSPECTIVE 191

    Judee Light 197

YOU DON'T HAVE TO SEE IT TO BELIEVE IT 198

    Sandra Champlain... 205

LIFE FROM HERE TO THERE 206

    Cindy Halley 212

WAKE UP TO THE UNIVERSAL GOD 213

    Steven E. Schmitt.. 216

I HAVE A GIFT FOR YOU! 217

    Lee Beard.. 220

HAPPINESS IS A CHOICE…IT IS YOURS TO MAKE 221

    Lorane Gordon.. 228

I FOUND HAPPINESS BY LEARNING THE TRUTH AND SHEDDING THE LIES 229

    Joe DiChiara... 236

FAILING FORWARD FAST FOR FINANCIAL FREEDOM 237

    Patricia Giankas.. 244

WHAT'S YOUR AMBITION? 245

    Doreen DeJesus 252

COLLABORATION: THE MODEL THAT WORKS IN THE 21ST CENTURY 253

    Dr. Paula Fellingham.. 259

HEY PROBLEM, YOU'RE MY FRIEND! 260

    Rev. Dr. David Laughray 265

A NOTE OF GRATITUDE.. 266

The Stories

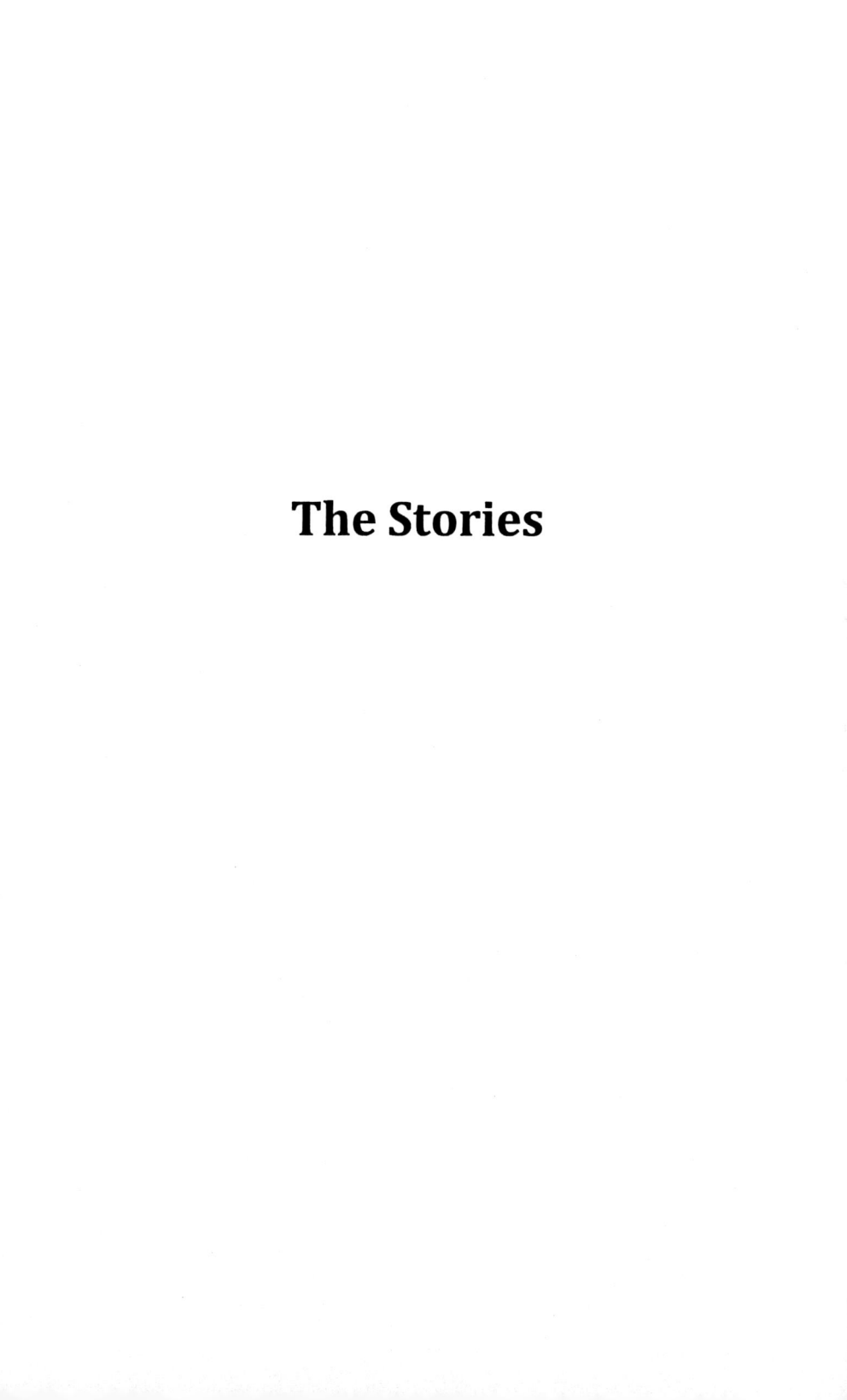

Break Down, Break Through, Break Free!

Burge Smith Lyons

D o you believe you have a choice in your life? Do you ever wonder why similar things keep "happening" to you over and over? Have you ever felt stuck, alone, or confused?

What if I told you that you have the power to change your reality? Would you believe me? This is my story about how I changed my reality by shifting my beliefs.

Break Down

I had been through one marriage, a bankruptcy, and had a child when I first began to teach workshops in 1993 on how to release the blocks in our lives and attract what we desire. I called these workshops *The Essence of Being* seminars. I was moved to develop these workshops so I could remind myself of what I had learned during my own personal growth before my life came crashing down around me. I knew that to really practice the principles I had to teach what I wanted to learn so they would become integrated into every fiber of my being.

Conversations That Make a Difference

In addition, I knew I was being watched by each person who participated in my public workshops. My life was under a microscope, and everyone knew every mistake I made. There was no way I could hide. I was under pressure to demonstrate for everybody just how these dynamic principles could change my life and the lives of everyone I taught. If I couldn't create the reality I wanted, then I believed they would think of me as an imposter which weighed heavily on me. I knew I had to shift the "imposter" issue for me to feel legitimate. Every time I stood in front of people and spoke, I thought to myself, "I believe what I am teaching is true, but I guess I'm not worthy of having 'it' or I would have 'it' by now." Everyone has a certain "it" that defines his or her success and happiness.

I taught principles such as "Law of Attraction," "Thoughts Create Reality" and how to release any old pain or thoughts that block us from getting what we want. I was helping others work through their emotional blocks while working on my own. I was telling people that they made a difference and to never give up on themselves or their dreams while my own personal life was not easy.

I was running my seminar business and learning how to be a mother with a new baby. I was having financial difficulty with my other business, and my marriage had problems. I was feeling guilty that I couldn't get myself out of this mess. I thought I should know better, because I was teaching this to other people. It seemed that no matter how hard I tried, I just couldn't get it right. I was emotionally beating myself up.

I knew that I "shouldn't" blame those around me or shame myself or make excuses for my life. I knew I was supposed to take responsibility for my thoughts, my beliefs, and my actions. Because I believed in a Higher Power, I knew that God/Universe had a purpose for me. I was being watched over by angels, yet I felt so alone. I felt helpless, tired, frustrated and impatient, and I kept asking myself, "If I'm on my path, shouldn't this all be easier? Shouldn't I be in the flow of things instead of hitting every rock in the river of life?" I "should" on myself a lot and it got messy.

I ended up getting a divorce and lost everything. No home, no business, no husband, and no money. Even during this time, I was teaching workshops. I believed that we can change our lives, and we have the power within us to make a difference. Ironically, the people who took my workshops wanted a change in their life too, just like me.

As a new beginning, I was left with a car with one headlight, one door that worked; no place I could call my own home, and a precious two and a half year old child to take care of by myself. I had several close friends who were more than willing to help me through this time, reminding me of who I really was and to never give in to becoming a victim. Despite their support, I still felt helpless and wanted to blame other people or myself for my problems. I knew that if I gave in to thinking I was a victim, my life would never change. I knew and taught people that when you blame yourself or others or make excuses, you are simply giving away your power. Then you really are stuck.

Through all of this transformation of my life, I was still hurting from the divorce and the bankruptcy. Everywhere I turned, I was reminded of the big red B on my forehead for bankruptcy and a huge scarlet D on my butt for divorce. From this point I became even more committed and driven to making a better life for my child. I knew I had to make it happen somehow.

Conversations That Make a Difference

I continued to teach and found my own place to live with my child. I realized as I practiced my own processes and exercises I had been teaching for a few years that I really didn't feel worthy enough to make a lot of money, be happy, or have a healthy, loving relationship. I was not attracting what my conscious thoughts were saying. My "Bubble Talk" or unconscious self-talk was, "I'm not worthy" and that trickled down into all of my spiritual, financial, emotional, mental and physical levels. "Bubble Talk" is the unconscious thoughts that keep us from getting what we want. Have you ever seen a cartoon character with a bubble over their head to show what they are thinking? They may be saying one thing, but thinking another. That is how our "Bubble Talk" works. If the conscious and unconscious minds are not aligned, it is harder to get what we want.

Break Through

I knew that I had to blow those bubbles away in order to create better bubbles. I had to break through my unworthy bubble and break through my victim consciousness. I kept myself surrounded by people that I loved and that loved me to remind me again of why I was here and what a difference I was truly making. I wrote visions and intentions of what I wanted. I created treasure maps and affirmations telling myself that I was indeed worthy, legitimate and deserved my heart's desire. When I processed people in the workshops with worthiness issues and helped them see their true nature, it helped me do the same.

I went on vision quests to help me gain clarity on what I really wanted so that I could attract it. I asked questions like: "Why me?" "What am I to do now?" "Show me the right path to take that will allow me to live in harmony and for the highest good." I created a "Healing Forest" around me and chose to walk the talk.

A "Healing Forest" is a Native American philosophy that describes people of like mind surrounding you to mirror the traits you desire. If you take a sick tree out of a sick forest, and nurture it back to health and stick it back into the sick forest, it could become sick again. In an ideal world, we take the sick tree out of the dysfunctional forest and create a healing forest around it so it can continue to flourish and thrive. I do not believe that any of us are sick and need healing; however, we do forget who we really are at times.

As I built a healing forest around me, I realized that my being stuck emotionally was a direct reflection of the dysfunction I grew up in. My mother, who had Multiple Sclerosis, was not only paralyzed from the pain of her illness, but also from the pain of enabling my alcoholic father. My life was a symptomatic metaphor for the environment I grew up in. One person at a time, I continued to build a healing forest around me.

In an effort to help children learn these lessons early on, I created a non-profit organization called, "The Healing Forest Foundation."

One of my many "Aha" moments came early in this process when I was looking for a new car. I'll never forget going to the Mercedes dealership with my old broken down Honda with one headlight to visualize my dream car. I parked a block away so the salesmen would not see what I really drove. I walked into the place like I owned it. I found myself touching and smelling the leather, sitting behind the wheel, visualizing myself driving this beautiful automobile. I was attached to it being this way and this particular car.

I held this dream for many years while continuing to blow away my unworthy bubbles (my beliefs), and they finally shifted. I attracted an opportunity to hone my theatrical and entrepreneurial background in the publishing sales industry and real estate. I remember when I received my first monthly check for $32,000. I was on top of the world. Finally! I had broken through my bubble. All of my inner work was beginning to pay off!

Break Free

As I continued teaching my transformational seminars, I created a network of thousands. I no longer needed to worry about creating income, and I continued to teach the workshops as I gave back to the community. I was using the sales business to support my workshop habit. I continued to flourish in all of my businesses.

I later attracted a powerful man that saw my true worthiness, and I could reflect back to him his own worthiness. We knew that we could create consciously together, and he was a perfect guide and father for my son. I had believed that I could create this perfect scenario, and I did! I finally went back to the Mercedes dealership to drive that "perfect" car and realized I really liked a Lexus I had driven even better and decided to buy the Lexus. I am not suggesting Lexus over Mercedes, but I am using this teachable moment to drive home the concept that being "attached" to any one thing, job, or relationship can block a person's success just as much as feeling unworthy. Once I let go of my attachment to the Mercedes, I allowed an even better alternative to come to me. I realized that when I get attached to something being a certain way or coming to me exactly the way I desire, it can sometimes set me up for disappointment or a limited experience. I've learned over and over that the more attached I am to something, the more rigid or limited my thinking becomes.

I noticed I was not really attached to the car, but the feeling of abundance and prosperity in my life. Once I got that loud and clear, things shifted again. I continued to create my desires with my visions, intentions, focus, and the belief that I am worthy and deserving while not being attached to a specific outcome. I now have both the Mercedes and the Lexus! The moral of this story is: let go of your attachment to having something manifest exactly the way you think it should, and you will be pleasantly surprised. Trust and allow; don't ask how!

By using these concepts that I teach, I have achieved millions in assets, a loving, conscious relationship and the opportunity to add value to others' lives by teaching these simple but profound principles.

My son is happy and has graduated from New York University. He has travelled the world getting paid doing what he loves as an actor. If I lost it all tomorrow, I know I could build it all again. I have evidence that believing in myself and shifting my "Bubble Talk" can make the difference between staying stuck and being a victim and getting unstuck and being a victor. I am a walking testimony that these principles work. No matter where you are in your life, you have a choice, just like I did!

Never give up on yourself and do not settle for a mediocre life. "You can have it all."

About the Author

Burge Smith-Lyons is a communications and relationship expert and president and CEO of Essence of Being, Inc., which has been offering personal and professional development programs for thousands of adults, families and companies from around the world for 21 years.

She is a motivational speaker, author, facilitator, minister, and trainer who specializes in helping people identify what she calls "Bubble Talk" — subconscious negative self-talk that blocks them from achieving what they want in life. Since 1981 she has been involved in her holistic mind-body-spirit approach which includes conscious breathing, kinesiology, emotional release, energy release, psychotherapy, NLP, EFT, anger-release work, channeling and Super Learning, accelerated learning techniques that activate both the left and right brain. Burge is chairman and founder of The Healing Forest Foundation, Inc., a non-profit organization that uses experiential learning to help children see their true gifts and how to express them through any challenges.

www.essenceofbeing.com
info@essenceofbeing.com
www.healingforestfoundation.org
Phone: 1-888-400-5566

Building Belief

Rita Davenport

In my senior year of high school, my home economics teacher, Mrs. Karleen Dean, who was also my guidance counselor, sat me down and told me the facts of life about my future.

"Forget about college, Rita," she said, "you're just not college material. My advice to you is to concentrate on finding a good husband."

I know that when I tell this story, that sounds awful. How could she say such a mean thing? But she wasn't being mean; the truth is she was right. I wasn't. I hadn't taken the preparatory classes — advanced math, trig, chemistry, things like that. What's more, in our generation, not all that many high school graduates went on to college, especially not among the women. Nobody in my family ever had, that's for sure. I didn't' really feel I had the academic aptitude to make college a likely track. And, Lord knew I didn't have the financial resources to pay for it. Mrs. Dean was only saying what made sense. There was no reason to believe that I could pursue a successful college career.

And that right there, that word, was the real issue: *belief.*

Conversations That Make a Difference

When Mrs. Dean said I wasn't college material, I believed her, and as a result, I deferred to her judgment. When my classmates started looking at what colleges they might apply to, I didn't pursue the thought at all. I just let it go. And if that had been that, you wouldn't be reading this story, because there would have been no story to write.

Mind your Mind

Most people think they think, but they don't actually think: they let other people think for them. If you don't choose what you think about, somebody else will choose it for you. Your thoughts are like your time: if you don't manage our time, someone else will manage it for you, and you'll live your life at the whim of others.

The capacity to truly think — to choose our own thoughts for ourselves — is an incredible gift that we've all been given by our Creator, and most of us never un-wrap the box, let alone take out what's inside and use it. Sue Grafton wrote this: *"Thinking is hard work, which is why you don't see many people doing it."* Albert Schweitzer was asked once, *"Well, I don't know. I just try to think once a day."* Once a day — and that put him way ahead of the rest of the world.

Buckminster Fuller, the man behind the geodesic dome and the ahead-of-his-time design slogan "do more with less" and one of the most brilliant men of the twentieth century experienced a great tragedy early in his life: his first child, a baby daughter, died from an illness. At the same time, he and his young wife were going through terrible financial struggles. Feeling like a complete failure, Fuller stood on the shore of Lake Michigan in the winter and was about to throw himself in — figuring that at least his wife could live off the

Shift Your Beliefs to Get What You Want

insurance money — when he suddenly stopped and made a radical decision; he decided to think.

Reasoning that he'd made a mess of his life by trying to follow other people's thoughts, he decided it was time to figure out what *he* though. For the next two years, he didn't speak a word: he wanted to make sure that when he opened his mouth, it would be his own thoughts that came out. And they were thoughts that changed the world.

I believe conforming to others' thoughts and ideas is one of the biggest strategic errors we can make. Conformity is the abdication of genuine belief: fitting yourself into people's expectations is a strategic error. You've got the answers buried in your right now.

A Change in Plans

My acquiescence to Mrs. Dean's assessment of my poor academic prospects did not last long. A few months after my high school graduation, I made the decision to put Mrs. Dean's advice aside. I decided I was going to college.

A big part of the reason I decided to put myself on track to a college career had to do with another person whom I believed in, specifically, a boy.

When I was fourteen, there was a boy in my freshman English class named David Davenport. I liked him right away. I like to joke that I had several guys waiting in the wings in case this one didn't work out, but it's not really true. David and I dated off and on starting our junior year. We went to our high school graduation together and after that we started dating seriously.

After graduating from high school I went looking for gainful employment. I was still working part-time at Woolworth's, Friday nights and Saturdays, and before long I found myself a regular weekday job, as I'll describe in a moment. At the same time, I was dating a college student, going to college ball games, and having regular glimpses of a kind of life that was very different from how I saw my own life would be like if I did not pursue a higher education.

David was a very motivating force for me. A serious and singularly determined student, he went through engineering school at Vanderbilt in only four years which was unusual, and graduated with honors. When he started, we would see each other one or two nights a week. By his senior year, we were lucky if it was once a week, because he was studying all the time. He was working really hard at getting that engineering degree, and I was in awe of him.

The fact that I was not in college gnawed at me. David and I were not engaged, but I knew he was the one I wanted to spend the rest of my life with. He was the kindest, smartest, best looking, sweetest, most intelligent person I had ever been around, and the person I felt I could trust and respect. I loved him, always have, always will and fully expected that I would marry him — and that posed a problem. You see, I figured that if I married a college graduate from Vanderbilt and did not have an advanced degree myself, it would not be long before he would outgrow me.

Instead, I wanted David to be married to someone he would be proud of, someone he had to run to keep up with. Someone who, someday, he would look at, poke the guy next to him with his elbow and say, "Hey, that's my lady up there on the stage."

I also wanted to be a significant person, because I was so proud of him. I believed in David, and that inspired me to believe in myself.

Shift Your Beliefs to Get What You Want

David encouraged and pushed me to make something out of myself. His mother was a single mom; she had lost her husband, gone to work, and always worked too. He would say to me, "What do you plan to do with your life?" No one had ever asked me that before!

It didn't take long. I pretty quickly decided that I had to go to college, too. I wasn't sure exactly what I would do with my life (to answer David's question), but most of the time, at that point, I thought I would probably become a schoolteacher, because so many teachers had inspired me over the years.

Sometimes my dreams were more grandiose. I remember telling David, "If you don't marry me, you'll be sorry. Someday I'm going to be a fashion designer, or open my own boutique..." (I always had a passion for fashion) "...and I'm going to be very successful." I'm sure he got a good chuckle out of that. Of course, I never did become a fashion designer or open any boutiques. Sometimes, when we're aiming for our biggest life dreams, the best we can do is approximate. And most times, that's good enough. Time and circumstance will fill in the details, as long as we provide the general aim, the passion, the elbow grease, and the sweat equity.

The Power of Belief

In my television interviews I would always ask people, "What do you think made you successful?" One of the most memorable times I asked that question was when I interviewed Muhammad Ali, and he told me about creating his famous affirmation, "I am the greatest," and how he used it to change his life.

In the beginning of his career, Ali was not all that great a boxer. He certainly wasn't *the greatest*. But he kept repeating

Conversations That Make a Difference

that positive assertion, that "I am" statement, as if the goal had already been achieved: I am the greatest. And in time he did indeed become the greatest boxer the world had ever seen.

Your mind only knows what you tell it. You can tell your mind that you're not going to be successful and you certainly won't be. Or you can tell your mind. "I am going to be successful *no matter what.*" That *no matter what* attitude is so key. When Ali used to say that, he wasn't boasting or bragging. He was exercising that *no matter what* attitude.

A woman named Phyllis came on my television show once and did a cooking segment. Phyllis had a unique brand of self-deprecating humor and she was very entertaining. She described herself as "ugly, divorced, with five children, almost no education, and living on welfare." However I knew there was more to the story, because she had actually become quite successful. I knew that at one time in her past, she had cleaned office buildings to get by, and I asked her about that, and about how she pulled herself out of that life to become so successful.

At night, she said, she would go around this one office building cleaning all the rooms. One night, she happened to see a book in one of the trashcans she was cleaning. The book was called *The Magic of Believing,* by Claude Bristol. She took the book home and devoured it.

"After I read that book," she said, "you know what? I was still ugly. I was still on welfare. I still had five kids. I was still divorced. But the book taught me one thing: quit comparing yourself to the beautiful people of Hollywood, because they don't exist."

Bristol's book told Phyllis, "*Protect your thoughts and turn them into achievements... Apply the power of your imagination to overcome obstacles."* It also urged the reader to find something she was good at, and become great at it.

"The only thing I could think of that I was good at," reported Phyllis, "was being funny. I'd always been told I was funny. I was voted wittiest in my high school. I thought, maybe I could go down to the local pub, after I finished cleaning up, and see if I could get on the microphone and tell a few stories and jokes. Hey, I'd do it for Fred." And that's exactly what she did. She started going down to that pub regularly after work and practicing her skill at telling jokes... and in time, Phyllis Diller earned millions for telling jokes. Like I've always said, "Being funny makes money!"

Twelve years later, in 1996, I was honored and humbled to be invited to Middle Tennessee State University once again, this time to give the university's commencement address for that year, where I would be addressing an audience of some 16,000 people. I invited Mrs. Dean, the teacher and guidance counselor who had thought that I was not college material, to join me in that event as well, and she did. We remained good friends until she passed away, June 20, 2013. I was grateful to nominate her and MC the program when McGavock High School named their school food service program in honor of Mrs. Dean.

Conversations That Make a Difference

About the Author

Rita Davenport has a unique background; she is an award winning speaker, humorist, and entrepreneur. Her career ranges from social work and teaching, to broadcasting, writing, and corporate management.

She is a charter member of the National Speaker's Association with the distinct recognition of CSP and CPAE and is listed in the National Speaker's Association Hall of Fame.

She has been featured in The Wall Street Journal, as well as National magazines such as *People, Networking Times, Success, and Working at Home*. She has received national recognition on radio and television shows.

Rita feels, however, that her most outstanding accomplishment is being a wife to her high school sweetheart David, a mother to her two sons, Michael and Scott, and "Nana" to her granddaughters, Reese, Claire Ray, and London.

As a speaker, Rita has been called: motivational, challenging, humorous, personal, and powerful! She's also known for speaking two languages…..English and Southern!!

www.RitaDavenport.com

Shift Your Beliefs to Get What You Want

Take Back Your Identity
Reclaim Your True Self to Become Your BEST

Dianne Reilly

When did you first think about who you are? What makes you "You"? Perhaps you grew up with a strong sense of your own personal identity. You were validated by two loving parents who knew what you would later need to thrive as an adult. If that is you, you are blessed. Perhaps you were the offspring of parents who were divorced, with or without a stepparent involved. You understand the brokenness which comes from a broken home. Perhaps you lost one or both of your parents at an early age and were raised by other family members or even foster care. Your last name may have been changed once or even several times in the process. The image you hold of yourself is strongly influenced at an early age by your family of origin.

So what does this have to do with identity? One of the first things you learn as a child is your own name, which becomes your identifier. When you hear your first name, something inside knows it means you! How was your name chosen? Were you named after a relative? Was your name chosen from the popular names of your era or after a movie star? If you were named after someone famous, did it make you feel special? Now, think about how you feel when someone says it wrong or calls you by the wrong name. It does feel personal, even if for a moment. A name is the first of many identifiers you take on in your life.

I would like to share some of my journey with you to give you hope that, no matter what your own journey has been up until now, you can reclaim the person you were born to be! The bumps in your road are only your experience; they no longer identify you. You are not your experience or your parent's experience. It doesn't matter what you went through or what you did as a result of it. Those things don't define you, they refine you. I have taken back my identity and so can you!

My mother named me after a song and sang it to me on the delivery table. She had a beautiful lyric soprano voice. I do not remember my father. Because of his drug/alcohol problem, she made the courageous decision to leave that life behind for my sake. I was only eighteen months old when she returned home to live with her parents. In doing so, all contact with my father's family was cut off. There is an entire side of my family heritage I know nothing about. I had my father's name but no father in my life.

Mother had an unsuccessful remarriage which gave me a brother and sister. My last name was legally changed to my stepfather's name so we would all have the same last name. A last name is an identifier in many cultures; it says to whom you belong; however, he did not adopt me. I was too young to understand the significance of this. As an adult, the message became clear in my mind — I was not good enough to adopt.

Shift Your Beliefs to Get What You Want

A child has a vivid imagination. I remember being five or six year old, thinking about a place somewhere in the distance that was not only beautiful but was a happy place. This occurred when I was in my stepfamily's environment. A child instinctively knows when he is not accepted. I was not in a happy place, so I created one.

When Mother's marriage unraveled, once again she and I went to live with my maternal grandparents. My brother and sister went to live with their father's parents to whom Mother had given temporary custody. The time spent with my grandparents provided me with stability, as well as acceptance and abundant love. We didn't have much, but it didn't matter. It was a safe place, a happy place, and many of the values I hold today were formed there. My grandmother taught me how to bake, cook, and sew. I also had a loving grandfather whom I adored. He was a strong, gentle giant in my life. He made me feel safe. He showed me that there are some great men in this world — hard working, undemanding. Although he was a quiet man of few words, people knew he was a man of great faith who lived what he believed.

When I was twelve, we moved again. Mother had saved her money. She wanted to create a new home for all of us as a family. She wanted to bring home my brother and sister. Although part of me understood, I cried for weeks because I didn't want to leave my happy place. This also meant yet another new school. Since I didn't have a choice, I became a team with Mother to help us build a new life. Because we were only fifteen minutes from my grandparent's home, we saw them frequently, thankfully.

During these years with my Mother, even while living with my grandparents, we became like sisters. We went downtown, went shopping, and to the movies. In a strange way, I felt as if I was her caretaker and I felt very protective of her. Perhaps, intuitively, I knew I could judge a person's authenticity better than she could. It was during those years I learned about control. My Mother was a young, beautiful woman who wanted to find a husband to assist her as she sought to rebuild her life and regain custody of her children. Occasionally, she met a man and brought him home to meet me. On each of these occasions, something in me rose up and I would defy him. The sweet, well mannered young lady I had become transformed into a monster! I was unfriendly and found ways to run off any potential suitor. Sadly, I probably ran off a nice one during this process. I developed an independent attitude and told Mother, "We don't need men in our lives." Also, I developed a belief that, if I could control the situation, I could prevent pain and disappointment. As life unfolded, I learned this belief was a lie.

My childhood and teen years were spent watching a relentless custody battle between Mother and her in-laws. Although Mother had a good job, she had costly legal bills, which meant we had very little money. Even during her marriage, we struggled financially. It was all I ever knew. When she regained custody of her children, the financial situation continued. The environment was stressful for all of us.

Growing up in a broken home, I felt I was different from other kids. This followed me into my teenage years. I was envious of others who lived in families with two parents. Sadly, I allowed the brokenness of my own family to become part of my identity. What we think and believe about ourselves affects how we pursue life. Even though I had friends and was in a high school sorority, I felt insecure about being from a broken home and having little money. I turned inward to keep from being rejected, avoiding pain at all costs.

Have you ever wanted to do something but because you didn't believe it was possible, you would not even try?

As a student, my grades were sufficient, but the chaos of my home life caused me to retreat, to mentally give up. I was not eligible for scholarships to universities. Mother was not knowledgeable in this area, but she gave me a book about college financial aid. My way of dealing with it? I simply said, "I don't want to go." I denied something I really wanted in order to maintain a sense of control.

Fortunately, my high school guidance counselor called me into her office to ask about my future plans. When I told her that I couldn't go to college because there was no money, she asked me if I would be willing to go to the local junior college if I could get a scholarship. Our local civic club gave away two scholarships every year and my grades were good enough to win. I only had to pay for my books. Of course I agreed. To my surprise, I won! As I went to the banquet to accept the award, it was the first time I won anything based on my own achievement. I will always be grateful to Mrs. Ann Riddle for her sensitivity and concern for me and for believing in me when I didn't believe in myself. This was a catalyst for a shift in my beliefs.

I finished my associate degree while working part time. Five years later, I returned to school as an adult, graduating with honors while working full time. I became focused on achievements, winning many sales awards in my company, and becoming very competitive. Looking back, I realized I had set out to prove to others that I had value and I could achieve. Perhaps I needed to prove this to myself. I believed awards could heal a broken place inside.

It took a crisis in my own life to make me aware that, over time, I had built such a wall around my heart that healing couldn't occur until it was removed. During a few short years, I received the promotion of my dreams and had earned my Bachelor's degree. This occurred while enduring my own marital crisis, the diagnosis of cancer in my mother, and her death a few short years later. These latter two events were the reason I sought counseling and were the start of my path to reclaiming my identity. During this time, I knew something was going to break. I resolved it would not be me. That is when I allowed the floodgates of my suppressed emotions to open, and I called out to God, my Heavenly Father, and asked for His help. I grew up in church, but I stopped going in my early teens and ignored my spirituality. I knew He was always there, but He loved me enough to wait for me to come to Him. That is when my healing began, for only God can heal a heart.

That is how I reclaimed my identity and set out to live my life with purpose. I am God's daughter. By finding my missing piece, my identity, I found my peace. I made a decision to forgive all those who had hurt me. I also forgave my father, who I don't remember, for his abandonment, for not being a part of my childhood, even from a distance. I discovered how much of an impact this abandonment had in my life and found healthy ways to fill that void and become whole again. I also gave up my desire for control. When that wall started chipping away, I felt vulnerable, but it felt good! It is only in our vulnerability that we can truly love, be of service to others and live out our purpose.

When in a life struggle, you can give up or you can go up a notch, it's your choice. If you don't know your identity, you may believe it is about your brokenness, your job, or your achievements and never discover who you were born to be. My prayer is that you choose to reach out and get what you need. Find a trusted advisor, pastor, or counselor to guide your journey to wholeness.

Today, it is my joy to help people discover their passion and purpose within themselves through the process of coaching. Through speaking, I am able to share my mess of a childhood as a message of hope. No matter what you have been through, you can be your BEST, which stands for Bold, Empowered, Strong and Thankful. Take Back Your Identity! You can do it! It is your birthright! May God bless you in your journey!

Conversations That Make a Difference

About the Author

Dianne Reilly is an honors graduate of Rollins College in Winter Park, Florida with a degree in Business Administration. After an award winning sales and management career of over twenty years with an international pharmaceutical company, she became an entrepreneur, owning several small companies. She is a member of the John Maxwell Team where she is certified as a Speaker, Trainer and Coach. She empowers entrepreneurs and businesses to achieve maximum levels of performance through leadership training and coaching. Dianne is also certified in the personal development program, Empowerment Mentoring, where virtual group classes and coaching provide the student a deeper undertaking into discovery, transformation and achievement. Dianne has a passion for assisting others to unleash and utilize their potential to the maximum. She is in leadership at her church and serves on several community boards in Central Florida.

Connect with her at:
diannereilly407@gmail.com
www.youridentitypower.com
www.JohnCMaxwellGroup.com/DianneReilly
www.EmpowermentMentoring.com/DianneReilly
https://twitter.com/LeadershipBEST

COURAGE - The Day I Found It
My Journey to Eckhart Tolle

Michele Penn

It began with a marriage filled with verbal torment. For fourteen years my ex-husband verbally abused my children and me until one day, in a wild, vicious rage, he threatened to kill me. That pivotal moment is when I finally found the courage to leave the marriage. Today, I have learned to forgive my ex-husband because that experience became the catalyst which changed my life. Instead of losing my life — I found it!

As I began my metamorphosis, for some unknown reason, the sight of flowers enthralled me. I felt the soul of each flower and was transfixed by its unique inner beauty. Where had they been my whole life? Why had I not seen them before?

When I read Eckhart Tolle's book, *A New Earth*, it taught me the importance of being present and awake. And while reading the very first chapter, *The Flowering of Human Consciousness*, I felt as if Eckhart was in my head. He explained, in a way I never could, why I was drawn to taking pictures of ONLY flowers. I was opening up to a new way of experiencing life. He touched my soul with his words. I had never been touched by words like that before. When I captured a moment of beauty in a flower, I experienced the spiritual awakening that Eckhart had described. Flowers intensified an awakening to my life's real purpose. A flower could do that? Yes. Flowers awakened me — and they can awaken you, too. I felt true joy, peace and happiness, and I began to realize that these feelings come from within. I was in the Present Moment and loving it. Eckhart reminds us, *"You are never more essentially, more deeply, yourself than when you are still."* When you are still, you can feel inspiration. When you quiet the constant chatter in your mind and allow yourself to just be, you can connect with your inner self, where all of your answers lie. Trust yourself, because you know more than you think you do.

Eckhart says, *"Those delicate and fragrant beings we call flowers would come to play an essential part in the evolution of consciousness of another species. Humans would increasingly be drawn to and fascinated by them. As the consciousness of human beings developed, flowers were most likely the first thing they came to value that had no utilitarian purpose for them, that is to say, was not linked in some way to survival. They provided inspiration to countless artists, poets and mystics. Jesus tells us to contemplate the flowers and learn from them how to live."* Wow.

Eckhart also says that, *"...seeing beauty in a flower could awaken humans, however briefly, to the beauty that is an essential part of their own inner most being, their true nature."* When he wrote that he was *"increasingly drawn to and fascinated by flowers,"* I understood exactly how he felt. I felt conscious without thought when I was photographing

Shift Your Beliefs to Get What You Want

flowers! It was the first time the chatter in my head stopped and I was still. The blame, guilt, resentment and anger left my head for an instant. The longer I photographed flowers, the longer I could stay in the present moment. It was so freeing.

Something Oprah Winfrey said came to mind: "Believe your thought and act upon it!" I knew my photographs of flowers were unique and spirit-filled. Then came an epiphany, a vision... I saw my photographs paired with Eckhart's quotes and I instinctively KNEW that he would connect with my flowers as profoundly as I connected with his words.

Acting on that thought, I designed a mock-up book of my photos paired with quotes from *A New Earth.* I then visualized and felt what it would be like to have this book on the shelves of Barnes and Noble. I wasn't wishing for this — I had a knowing deep within me that the book already existed! I lived as though it were already done.

Synchronistic events began to occur in my life. At a conference, I ordered a candle to be shipped to my home, and when it arrived it was the wrong color. I called the woman who sold it to me at the conference and left her a message. When she called me back, she said, "Everything happens for a reason." I believe that as well, but couldn't imagine what the reason was for this error. As we continued our conversation, we talked about our lives, spiritual paths, and my dream to have the book of photos and quotes from Eckhart Tolle's book, *A New Earth*, come to life.

It was then that the "reason" for the call revealed itself. The woman told me that she had written a book and, believe it or not, her publisher had just published a children's book

Conversations That Make a Difference

with Eckhart Tolle. My connection to Eckhart Tolle manifested itself because of this telephone conversation.

This wonderful woman then offered to contact her publisher to see if he would be open to hearing about the book. A few days later, she confirmed with me that I could indeed email some photos and my idea to the publisher, Bob Friedman. Because he was doing this as a favor, she asked me to keep my message short and sweet as he was very busy with "manuscripts from floor to ceiling to review."

I sent Bob Friedman an email describing my vision. Although he loved what I had to say, said it was a great idea and loved my work... he also said that we could never get Eckhart Tolle to agree but would be happy to put me in touch with other spiritual authors. However, my inspiration, vision, dreams and passion was the connection to Eckhart Tolle. I told Bob that if we could just get Eckhart Tolle to look at my work, I KNEW that he would feel the same inspiration and passion that I did.

Instead of mailing the mock-up, as Bob suggested, I asked if I could fly up and meet with him so I could present my "vision" in person. I wanted to see his face when he opened the book. He agreed and we decided on a time when the CEO would be there as well. After my meeting with Bob, he called in the CEO and the marketing director, and they all loved the mock-up. Again, they reiterated that it was a LONG SHOT to get Eckhart Tolle to even look at my book, but since I was so inspired and determined, and they really loved my book, they agreed to send it to Eckhart's publisher, Namaste. If the publisher's at Namaste loved it, and "only" if they loved it, they would show it to Eckhart Tolle.

Weeks and months went by. Because I was manifesting that it was already DONE, I didn't once question whether

Shift Your Beliefs to Get What You Want

Eckhart would get to see the mock-up, or whether he would like it. And then the phone call came in from Bob Friedman. He said, "I am in shock, but because of your genuine spirit, passion and belief, we are on second base. Namaste loves it and has agreed to show it to Eckhart Tolle." I never for one minute doubted that this would happen!

After some time, I received a phone call that Eckhart loved the idea too!! He wanted to do the book with me!! I was very excited but, because my belief was so strong in knowing that it was DONE, the news didn't surprise me! My friends and family, on the other hand, were shocked and impressed. They couldn't believe that I could manifest something like this. I was living my purpose and on my way.

Eckhart said he wanted to include Byron Katie in the book as well, which was another wonderful happening. I eagerly signed the contract and was told that the book was due out later that year. But, four months later, I got a phone call from the CEO of Hampton Roads telling me that they had decided not to print the book. He said that they were canceling the contract because of the economy — that it wasn't financially feasible to do a four-color book.

When I got off the phone, I was disappointed but didn't get upset. I knew this was just part of the journey because the book was already DONE. With my belief in tow, I called the CEO back a few days later and had an incredibly positive conversation. I talked about how the world needed to be inspired by this great combination of quotes and flowers. I talked from my heart and soul. I explained to him that I was so sure he would change his mind, which a few minutes ago I had purchased the website page "Peace in the Present Moment" because I knew this was going to benefit the world. And then... he agreed! We were back on track and the contract was renegotiated. *Peace in the Present Moment* was published in October 2010.

I never met Eckhart Tolle during this whole process. In June 2012, I attended his retreat at The Omega Institute in Rhinebeck, NY. Eckhart spoke for days, and I loved every minute of it. He was enlightening, funny, motivating and inspirational. The first night I tried to talk to someone who could get me to see Eckhart, to no avail. I finally spoke to Eckhart's manager, who told me that he doesn't see or speak to anyone personally at conferences. They keep him very protected, he rarely does book signing and I was told that press interviews are virtually impossible to schedule.

My persistence paid off when Eckhart's manager finally agreed to ask him if he would meet with me privately. I gave a copy of Peace in the Present Moment to his manager so that Eckhart would know who I was. The next morning, he told me that he didn't want to bother Eckhart last night because he had been too tired, but said he would try again that evening.

The following day I heard someone call my name. I looked around and saw Eckhart's manager over a sea of 500 people. I waved to him. He came up to me and said Eckhart would love to meet me at the end of the conference. Of course! I knew it would be an incredible experience.

At noon on a Wednesday — a day I will never forget — I was escorted into Eckhart Tolle's room. Eckhart wanted to hear my story from start to finish, wondering how I was able to "miraculously" (his word) get to him. It was an incredible 40 minutes. Eckhart thanked me for creating our book! How amazing. He hugged me for what felt like five minutes. It was a dream come true. We signed one another's books and took some pictures and then he asked me to sign a book for

Shift Your Beliefs to Get What You Want

Oprah, because he was going to be seeing her soon and wanted her to have a copy. That was another dream come true! We all know how much Oprah loves Eckhart Tolle!

Today, I continue to manifest amazing things into my life. I attracted the man of my dreams by using the law of attraction and the power of the present moment. And, I am living the life I always imagined ... knowing full well that all of us can be "awakened to our life's passion and purpose." I have found mine – have you found yours?

My purpose now is to inspire and encourage each of you to live the magnificently happy and fulfilling life that you deserve. Dreams do come true. And most importantly, the past doesn't define you. If I could go from a verbally abused woman and feeling powerless to collaborating on a book with two New York Times best-selling authors, then imagine what you could do? My book with Eckhart Tolle and Byron Katie, *Peace in the Present Moment* (Hampton Roads Publishing, October 2010) was the result of a journey to presence and to finding my life's passion and purpose. "Believe it, Feel it, Become it!"

About the Author

Michele Penn is an author, inspirational speaker, award winning photographer and creator of the book *Peace in the Present Moment* with New York Times best-selling authors Eckhart Tolle and Byron Katie. She lives in Sarasota, Florida, with David, the man of her dreams. Michele was raised in Short Hills, New Jersey, attended Millburn High School and graduated with a bachelor's degree from Syracuse University. Her three beautiful children, Freddy, Nicole and Melanie, fill her life with inspiration.

In the book, *Peace in the Present Moment*, Michele Penn's breathtaking floral photographs add peace and a deep stillness to the wisdom of Eckhart Tolle and Byron Katie. Michele's close-up photos, her "soul shots" are a symbol of enlightenment. With her second book, *Dance in the Garden*, Michele combines her "soul shots" with quotes from some of the most influential people of our time.
www.PeaceInThePresentMoment.net
www.Facebook.com/PeaceinthePresentMoment
(115,000 likes on Facebook)
http://peaceinthepresentmoment.net/abused-to-awakened/

Clearing the Clutter to Clarify Your Mission™

Alexandra Figueredo

Here I was, the "Missionpreneur Mentor," and I just couldn't get my own life together. How was it that despite talking to my clients about clarifying *their* missions, that *I* was unclear and stuck in my own chaos — chaos I created myself?

This certainly included physical clutter, between stacks of files and unopened mail littered about and useless knickknacks strewn around. Then it became evident that clutter had permeated into other personal and professional areas as well. Always known as the diplomatic and stable one among my family and friends, I was finding myself constantly irritated and angry with my business, relationships, family members, clients, and worst of all, with myself.

So just how did the "diplomatic and stable girl" get here, surrounded by mess, living paycheck to paycheck, arguing with overly dramatic family members and clients, and in an emotionally abusive relationship, all at the same time?

My journey had certainly not been linear. Growing up, I was a born musical performer, excelled in school, had many friends and delighted the adults. The only sticking point I got in trouble for was "being messy" — specifically having a disorganized bedroom or not picking up after myself at home. My mom, who has Type-A tendencies, used to yell and call me "messy" as a child, and it became easier to accept that as the truth rather than argue.

It isn't a surprise then that I grew up believing "messy" was inherently part of me. In my mind, my mom's neat craze was a neurosis, and I told myself, "My mess is no big deal. There are far more important matters, and besides, it's only one fault." Sure enough, my "fault" didn't prevent me from leading a functioning, successful life into adulthood.

As I stepped into college and planned my future, finance became the stable and lucrative industry of choice. Eager and ambitious, I embarked on a banking career that lasted for nearly a decade and was continuously promoted up the corporate ladder. It was around the time the economy tanked in 2008 that I felt something was missing and realized I wasn't living my true calling.

Embracing this renewed self-discovery, within the year I began my master's in communications and resigned to work with a startup business helping artists. Although it was meaningful work, it quickly became evident I was becoming a struggling artist myself. Adapting quickly, I expanded my business to work with what I call *missionpreneurs*, social entrepreneurs passionate about making a difference in the world, and willing to invest in my services. Thus my company, Mission Based Branding Institute, was born as a platform to help *missionpreneurs* clarify their mission, develop their brand and promote their mission and message.

Business finally started taking off. Soon, however, I began attracting dramatic situations and people around me. There were never-ending soap operas in my home, relationship, clients, family interactions and finances. Plus I was sick and tired all the time. This was certainly not the lifestyle I pictured doing my life's work.

For the first time, it became glaringly obvious how detrimental my ever-present "mess" was in my life as an entrepreneur. To be successful as one's own boss, one has to create structure and systems and must be extraordinarily disciplined. These had been my weaknesses, ones I had gotten away with in the corporate world due to built-in structure and bureaucracy. Furthermore, there was constant disarray in my home and office from piles of papers and files thrown everywhere to the mini-dramas I allowed into my life on a daily basis. My personal baggage was producing turmoil and pain, in the form of arguments, bounced checks, lost clients, and other missed opportunities.

It was then a revelation appeared through the guidance of a trusted mentor: this clutter and chaos had become a convenient excuse for not moving forward in my life. It was an excuse for not seeing clearly, for remaining stagnant, for not pursuing goals, for not playing full out, and ultimately for not living up to my calling. I was inadvertently sabotaging my progress, my goals and my success by choosing to remain surrounded by baggage — physically, emotionally and spiritually. The chaos was a decades-long manifested form of my fear and insecurity.

The saddest part was I wasn't fully pursuing my mission even though I thought and said so. I proactively chose to overcome this over months of reflection, meditation, therapy, focused action and support from loved ones to let go of my baggage and step into my greatness. This created a mindset shift. Now, rather than worry or complain about the chaos and drama when it popped up, I began to ask questions. How can I most serve others? How can my environment best support me? How can I positively focus my attention to increase wealth? Who can I help that will value me and my services? From then on, I resolved more than ever to pursue my mission to inspire, educate and promote *missionpreneurs* to share their message with the world in a bigger way.

Proactively choosing to organize my life created harmony and order in my thoughts. With sharper vision, it became easier and less stressful to fire the overly dramatic, underpaying client and end the abusive relationship. For once in my life, I also chose to say yes to organization in my personal environment because I wanted to, not because I was forced to or felt guilty about it.

Clear the clutter in multiple areas of your life and you can remove many of the disruptions and blinders that may be sabotaging your success. These distractions compiled over time can create the turmoil or "fires" you often see on a daily basis. A common example is the frenzy you feel when you lose your keys while rushing to leave for an important client meeting. Cleaning up and creating systems to eliminate as many of these diversions as possible can free you up to spend more time focusing on your mission and goals.

Why should you care about your mission anyway? Your mission is the fuel that drives you and your business forward. No matter how great your car is working, if you run out of fuel — the passion, purpose and motivation in your business — you're going to sputter until you eventually come to a stop. Without a strong mission, what on earth are you working toward? We all know profit alone cannot be your sole driving force. Besides, people won't remember you or your brand for being the most profitable business; rather they're going to remember how you made them feel, how you cared and how you gave back to the community. Having a strong mission attracts others who are aligned and emotionally engaged with your vision and who are loyal and endorse you and your brand.

What are some ways that you can remove the clutter in your life and help clarify, refine and reignite your mission? I developed what I call the CLARITY Process. CLARITY is an acronym for the following steps:

- **C**hoose
- **L**ist
- **A**ct
- **R**eflect
- **I**ntention
- **T**rust
- **Y**ield Results

First, let's apply the CLARITY Process to decluttering your life, clearing the physical, emotional and spiritual baggage, as follows:

1. **Choose**: Decide it's time to release and remove the clutter in your life.

2. **List**: Write the top three areas in your life currently attracting the most pain, negativity or distraction. These can be people, objects, habits, thoughts or behaviors.

3. **Act**: This week eliminate one piece of clutter or take one positive step in each of the three areas. Make it a point to take one additional step in each area each week for the next month.

4. **R**eflect: Meditate and journal on your trouble areas. How has your baggage been holding you back? Have you been bringing similar types of drama into more than one area of your life?

5. **I**ntention: Resolve and commit to do whatever it takes to break through and release what's holding you back.

6. **T**rust: Have faith in the process and believe in your abilities.

7. **Y**ield Results: As you dump whatever is holding you back and free up space in your life, welcome in renewed openness and tranquility.

Once you're aware of what's keeping you stuck, this process will help tremendously to reverse and ultimately reduce the chaos. Try the CLARITY Process whenever you need it for one day, one week, one month or a whole year!

Next you'll want to utilize the CLARITY Process to discover and/or refine your life's purpose and mission:

1. **C**hoose: Make the decision that you are open to pursuing your mission and new opportunities.

2. **L**ist: Name three areas you are currently most passionate about. They could be interests, hobbies, talents, causes, volunteer groups, etc. What is it that has been stirring up in your heart? Have you been hesitating or waiting on some project? Ask the Creator, "How can you best use me? How can I best serve?"

3. Act: This week choose one positive step you can take to move toward your mission in each of the three areas. What are your goals? Can you tie in any of your passions to your work or brand? Can you volunteer at a charity you love, or create your own? Be creative and don't limit your possibilities.

4. Reflect: If you're having a hard time getting clear, pray, meditate or journal for 5-10 minutes per day for up to a month. Be still and write whatever answers come to mind.

5. Intention: Align yourself and resolve to reignite the passion and purpose in your life and to tie that in to your life's work or calling.

6. Trust: Have faith and believe you are on the purpose-driven path toward your greatness.

7. Yield Results: Open yourself to receive blessings and opportunities in your life.

The CLARITY Process is powerful. To share a timely experience, I made a point to do spring cleaning a few months ago to clear out baggage and welcome new opportunities. Having recently interviewed a Mission Chat Show podcast guest that had been part of several collaboration books, I began focusing on becoming a collaborative author to share my message. Less than a week after cleaning, the opportunity for this book project suddenly appeared, and it turned out to be even better than I ever imagined! The CLARITY Process illuminated the path toward contributing to this book.

With openness in your heart and a revived sense of passion, you will begin moving closer to living a purposeful and mission-driven life in 30 days. Many of my clients who have gone through this process feel lighter, and more focused and determined than ever. For those *missionpreneurs* that need additional help clarifying their mission, I've worked one-on-one to zero in on the many facets of their purpose and mission and then tie that to their life's work and brand.

Whenever you feel the chaos start up again, use the CLARITY Process to help declutter your life and calm the disorder. Declare that chaos no longer takes over your life. Rather than spend excess energy or worry on your drama, be still and place your trust and faith in the Creator or your higher calling and mission.

We are not meant to live in complacency and mediocrity. Getting caught up in self-sabotaging behavior holding you back does not allow you to live up to your greatness. Eliminating the physical, emotional and spiritual clutter frees up space in your life for the right people, clients, resources and opportunities that will steer you closer to your purpose-driven path.

Align with those opportunities and step up with the courage to pursue your mission, your calling and your magnificence. Declare "I am up for the challenge" and step up and go. NOW is your time to step into that revived sense of purpose and greatness the Creator has rightfully birthed in you. If not NOW, when?

About the Author

Alexandra Figueredo, aka *Missionpreneur Mentor*, is founder of Mission Based Branding Institute, a full-service communications agency and training platform dedicated to helping mission-driven businesses. She's also a speaker, writer and host of Mission Chat Show podcast. Prior to her communications career, Alexandra worked in the finance industry for nearly a decade, most recently as an officer at a bank in Miami. During her years in the corporate world, she realized her legacy was to give back to others, which drove her to follow her mission and ultimately create her own company.

She is particularly passionate about giving back to causes that use arts and therapeutic means to help underserved youth. In 2011, she released her first book *Sculpt Your Life From Sketch to Masterpiece™*, a practical and inspirational guide helping readers discover their mission and create a mission-driven business and life. Contact her at www.missionbasedbranding.com, alexandra@missionbasedbranding.com
@OnAMissionAlex on Twitter.

Claim Your Truth

Linda Satya Tsai

We all wade through life with adopted, hand-me-down beliefs from our families and society. These beliefs make up the perpetual contexts of our internal and mostly unconscious dialogue, and lay the foundation to our experiences in life. Our beliefs cause us to think and make decisions that either support or suppress our personal power. They are rooted in our subconscious mind and we just need awareness to be able to shift them. The first step in shifting limiting beliefs is to identify those which are holding us back and systematically reprogram them.

With awareness, we can consciously shift our perspective beyond old belief paradigms into new worlds of possibilities. Choosing beliefs that support us to function at greater levels, naturally guide us towards who we want to be and are capable of becoming.

Anything is Possible

Much of our discomfort in life comes from some form of incongruence within ourselves. The parts of ourselves and our lives that don't feel good are beckoning us to listen and align ourselves to our deeper truths, ones that guide us to live on purpose. It gives us the opportunity to choose beliefs that will support our best possible outcomes.

I started out my life as a Pollyanna, someone with the belief, "anything is possible." I believed I could achieve anything I set my mind to, and I did! I could share countless stories of synchronicity and fabulous achievements that have been the magical tapestry of my life for more than twenty years. I travelled the world, achieved success in virtually every field I played in, lived in my dream home with driver and domestic helper, was featured in top international magazines and have been an industry leader and speaker. I've had the privilege of transforming hundreds of lives. I am convinced that my strong belief of anything is possible helped sway life in my favor.

Imagine that who we want to become and what we want for our lives is being created by our beliefs. Quantum physics shows us that we have a direct impact on that which we focus on, by virtue of observing it. I know that's a bit of a mind-twister but think of it this way: knowing this helps us focus on positive beliefs to help us attract the possible outcomes we want. When we begin the practice of shifting our energy and focusing on beliefs that support our visions, we begin to enjoy the magic of life's possibilities as they unfold for us, producing richer and far more fulfilling experiences.

Break the Spell of Limiting Beliefs

Getting caught in the spell of limiting beliefs can happen to the best of us. I've gone from living my wildest dreams to becoming completely stuck, back to living my dreams by virtue of what beliefs I choose to focus on. To many, living a life full of dreams would be like winning a lottery ticket. Having been on both sides of the spectrum I can share this, it's entirely possible to move beyond our limiting beliefs and to go through life making our visions a reality…and to do so with confidence.

Despite great successes, I was wrought with limiting beliefs about starting over in the US after ending my 17-year marriage and a chapter of life abroad in Asia. For the first time in my life I felt paralyzed by fear; fear of not being good enough, fear of failure; I even feared the best was behind me. It was a time of great reflection and an opportunity to dismiss beliefs that were keeping me from my highest potential. It helped me get in touch with my truths, as well as beliefs that were going to support a fabulous vision for my future.

Once I broke the spell of those limiting beliefs and remembered that magic beyond my wildest imagination is possible, I was present to a new relationship with myself by the internal dialogue I was having. Once again I was for myself, my life, and for things working out. Feeling stuck can actually be an opportunity to audit your life and transcend unfavorable beliefs that are not creating the results you want. It is also an opportunity to strengthen a more positive, kinder internal dialogue with yourself.

Most of our limiting beliefs are habitual and our practice is to replace them with empowering beliefs that put us back in our truth. The moment you feel dis-empowered is your invitation to reprogram that belief or thought which is not supporting you to one that does. It is not difficult. It simply takes awareness, practice and repetition until it becomes natural.

The Power in Our Truths

Consider that many of your limiting beliefs may be nothing more than distorted thoughts and realities you have consciously or unconsciously accepted. I learned the irony behind our limiting beliefs during an event with peak performance coach Anthony Robbins. We were asked to write down our dominant limiting belief and the truth about it. He clued us in that the exact opposite was our truth. I wrote, "I don't have what it takes", and my truth was, "I always exceed my own expectations." WOW! Liberating! I found the same pattern with the rest of my limiting beliefs! It was very empowering to discover far more wonderful beliefs behind my false beliefs that had started impacting my ability to move forward after my divorce.

As a life coach, I work with people who are ready to take their lives or business to the next level and it is natural for them to bump up against their limiting beliefs, where things such stress or doubt can take over their experience. Armed with what I know about limiting beliefs, it doesn't take long to help them discover the power in their truths to start creating their dream life.

Try the exercise for yourself. Discover the power in your own positive truths to move past the constraints of your mind and start living the life of your dreams!

Adopt Beliefs That Elevate You

Stepping up in life greatly depends on adopting beliefs that will elevate you. The moment we begin to move beyond our limiting beliefs, it's as if life's possibilities flow to us effortlessly. When we begin to believe in ourselves, synchronicity and opportunities unfold, guiding us closer to our higher purpose and rightful path. When we begin choosing beliefs that support our best life, we are much closer to seeing, feeling, hearing and knowing our higher callings.

Start adopting beliefs that focus your energy on possibilities that elevate you, and make you feel good. It doesn't make sense to pay attention to beliefs that are not supporting us, and probably aren't even true. "Police and Release" them. We want beliefs that ground us in our truths and move us toward our life purpose.

Take inventory of your beliefs for the purpose of understanding which ones propel you toward your life's work and identify those that keep you playing small.

Adopting new empowering beliefs is like being at home with the world and feeling safe. They will help you tap into possibilities and your personal power. Start practicing and have fun creating beliefs that put your perspective back in the world of magical possibilities.

Expect the Best

We have heard time and time again that the answers are within us, and yet some of those answers remain elusive. We want to find answers that make us feel passionate, motivated, and inspired about what we do. Try on the possibility that your visions of the future may hold answers for you. We take these visions for granted. Consider the possibility that when you saw the vision, it may have already happened somewhere in time. Your visions hold clues about what is possible for your future. Take Walt Disney for example. When he saw his vision for *Disneyland*, it wasn't a question of "if" it would happen, but rather of "when" it would happen.

Shift Your Beliefs to Get What You Want

These visions quite possibly could be the seeds of our potential waiting to be claimed. We have a responsibility to our highest potential to release dis-empowering beliefs that inherently stray us from our purpose. Find the beliefs that resonate as your truths and start b-e-l-i-e-v-i-n-g. Hedge your bets on beliefs like "Expect the best" or "I have what it takes."

Some of us may worry about not having complete clarity or certainty entering into new situations. We can easily become overwhelmed with possible negative outcomes, when positive outcomes are just as likely. When that happens, it's an invitation to look at the belief and ask ourselves, "Is this serving me or not?" "Is it making me feel good or bad?" Simply put, if it's making you feel bad, it's time to get busy reprogramming! Your personal power lies in the ability to claim empowering beliefs to create or attract what you want. The power is strongest when you expect the best.

Nourishing New Beliefs

Our brain is an incredible recording device that does not always know what is true or not. When you see a scary scene in a movie, you react as if it is happening to you versus on the screen. In life we are reacting very much the same way to our unconscious limiting beliefs that feel so real. Discovering our limiting beliefs is an opportunity to get very honest with ourselves and recognize those that haven't been serving us and are holding us back. We can look at them through the heart of compassion and even with a sense of humor, realizing that we have the ability to choose empowering beliefs that are just as possible. Although it might be helpful to understand where our limiting beliefs come from, what's more important is how we are going to consciously reprogram them.

Conversations That Make a Difference

I find people who are the most peaceful and happiest have beliefs about themselves and the world that support them having a wonderful experience of life, despite their circumstances. I also find these people have a great degree of success or luck. It seems that the beliefs at the foundation of their thinking just might cause them to have these desired effects in their lives.

If our beliefs are creating much of our reality, we can start aligning our beliefs which we now hold as truths somewhere in our DNA, gut, heart, wherever it may be for you, perhaps in every bone, fiber, and cell in your body. We can get so overwhelmed by our false limiting beliefs that we lose sight of the truths within us, that part of us we call intuition that holds answers for us.

Seeing this is a wonderful gateway to welcome in and nourish new beliefs that will help us reach higher levels of existence and connection with our spiritual purpose. Choose to reprogram beliefs that make your soul shine brightest – and watch you light the way for others!

The Joy of Living Fully

Truth is a word that has come up very strongly for me over the past few years. Even the spiritual name that found me, Satya, means truth in the Sanskrit language. Be open to the beliefs that are calling you to have faith in what you see, feel, hear and know as your own truths.

When you shift your limiting beliefs to empowering beliefs, watch the magic and momentum unfold like a synchronistic symphony of new people and opportunities that you hadn't considered possible. Having the life experiences we want comes down to adopting beliefs that support our enjoying life more. We can then watch the magic of our empowering beliefs play out rather than wasting our time in worry.

Discovering truths beyond your limiting beliefs will set you free to embrace the plethora of possibilities available. Enjoy reprogramming beliefs that support the realities you choose for your life. In the process you will have become a suitable friend to yourself, one who chooses beliefs which support the joy of living fully. It's exhilarating to watch my clients awaken from their limiting beliefs, and step out, front and center on the stage of their best life. Now it's your turn, adopt beliefs rooted in your truths and begin creating magic in your life!

About the Author

Linda Satya Tsai is an award-winning entrepreneur with over ten years' experience as a pioneer and industry leader in Hong Kong's fitness nutrition field. For almost twenty years she has been enthusiastically empowering people to reach their highest potential.

Satya is a motivational speaker and facilitator. She has been a featured life coach and entrepreneur on TV & radio, in international newspapers and magazines such as *Marie Claire*, and columnist for publications such as *Women's Health*.

Satya's personal passion to learn everything that speaks to optimum health, personal growth, and professional success, led her to discover her life's purpose of helping others transform physically and psychologically.

She has helped hundreds to implement their full potential to achieve amazing results. It is her greatest joy in life to support those who are ready to believe in and achieve their dreams.

Armor of Wisdom

Deidre Trudeau

B lasting down the highway I noticed a woman walking at an odd pace on the left shoulder near a parked SUV with its flashers on. Then I noticed a man way out ahead of the SUV walking the same way but he was staring intently down on the ground. "Aaaa, they are looking for something," I thought, then instantly imagined the whole scenario — she had angrily tossed her diamond ring out the window. I wondered how I came up with that conclusion so quickly and was immediately transformed thirty years earlier remembering impulsively flinging my wedding ring into the ocean. What was REALLY interesting to me about that memory was that I distinctly recalled thinking, "NO, I should have at least saved it to hock for a half month's rent in case of an emergency."

Allowing myself to sink further into that distant memory, I recalled just hours after my faithful 'ring toss' a shattering sequence of events unfolded. Tremendously distraught over some personal issues, I had stolen away overnight one weekend to the ocean in order to clear my head. This would be the first time I had spent a night away from my daughter since having her two years before, and the first time my husband would be solely responsible for her. We were having serious issues and I came to regret having married at only nineteen in an effort to avoid being a single mom. Sadly, as it turned out, being a single mom would have been the very least of my worries.

Sitting on that cool New England sand after tossing my ring, I stared out at the expansive sea, praying, seeking for guidance and thrashing through anxious and fear driven thoughts. The road had been so emotionally wrenching up until then and I knew full well a divorce was only going to turn up the heat. My gut wrenching thoughts could not have prepared me for what I was to find and experience when I returned from my ocean sojourn; our apartment empty and my husband and two year old daughter were nowhere to be found.

My husband had kidnapped my daughter and harbored her for over five weeks. I became a wild-eyed, crazed train wreck glued to the police station throughout the entire time. My shattered emotions quickly amplified from anguish to rage after she was found, because the authorities felt it necessary to remove her immediately from both our care and place her into temporary protective foster care until they could work out the details. I was beyond outraged for that alone but in addition; no criminal charges had been brought against my husband. Feeling alone, betrayed, traumatized and totally petrified for my daughter's well being I started begging anyone who would listen and clawed my way through the system until I was able to gain supervised visitation and eventually temporary custody of my daughter. The divorce and following years were wrought with exhausting and heated battles eventually ending in my ex-husbands despondency and disinterest in the welfare of our daughter's life. The only reason he was fighting at all was to avoid paying child support. I finally gained full custody and gladly relinquished all financial responsibility from him for child support, something that would prove to become a challenge later. I quickly put 3,000 miles between us and that horrific nightmare. My daughter and I left the Northeast for California in 1990, sight unseen in a 1983 Dodge Omni hatchback.

I crashed and burned my way through the next 30 years desperate to mask the shame, humility and disappointment over so many things. Mounting regrets seemed to build into deep insecurity, reducing my life into little more than the sum of my grievances and pain. So disappointed my life had not come close to the way I had dreamed it would go. And though I was able to pursue a life career in creative art and design, my optimism, joy and spirit was at an all time low. I had lost myself, my focus and my way. How could I regain my joyful essence and tap more deeply into my inherent sacred truth and power?

I had thought the pain and discomfort of past regrets would eventually subside and heal, but they did not. Shivers sliced down into my spine and soul every time I thought of the things I had to be regretful over. Why was I unable to get past it all? I tried everything...I eagerly learned about meditation, visualization, positive affirmations, setting intensions, journaling, tapping into intuition, actively being present, immersed myself in art, yoga, music, gardening and fitness. Something was just not clicking. What was I missing or holding onto that was no longer serving me? How was I supposed to process and heal from it all? I knew inside I was a spirited, creative, loving, caring and well meaning soul, determined to lead an industrious and enjoyable life. I was clearly searching. Then one day I saw an interview with Pastor Rick Warren about his best-selling book *The Purpose Driven Life,* he stated, *"Everyone's life is driven by something — and if you live for the approval of others, you will die by their rejection."* That blew me away. Who was I trying to please or get approval from all these years and why? And how much of that was causing my disappointment, led by ego and the tortured perception of not measuring up?

I continued to allow mistakes and failures to lull me into an even darker place. My greatest effort and earnest dreams left unfulfilled. What a blow to the ego! My expectations shattered. I gave it my all and repeatedly failed. It started to wear on me so much it scared my soul, dulled my spirit and weakened my power. At first it took its toll on my confidence but later it continued to wedge its way into my overall state of mind, my health and collective spirit. It crushed the lifelong perception of me. I felt defeated and my world continued to narrow, growing dim and heavy. I knew something HAD to give, I had to dig deep, peel back the layers, get real, grounded and reunited with my spirit and soulful place of connection and knowing. What was I not seeing or unwilling to accept?

One day I found the following quote:

"Forgiveness does not change the past, but it does enlarge the future." ~ Paul Boese

Wow! I started to wonder what it would be like if I forgave myself. What would my life be like and how would I feel. How would it be if I no longer resented myself and others? It wasn't until then I realized it was totally possible to mindfully SHIFT into a place of acceptance and forgiveness. I challenged myself to awaken, recognize and break free from nagging resentments and the regrets I had become so comfortably addicted to? Yes, I could do this. I simply had to imagine and immerse myself into the sensation of it all, the freedom born of forgiveness, self respect and confidence. And this time it was in no way going to be about me it was about why, defining a purpose that is far greater than me.

Desperate and humbled I craved the valuable insights and wisdom of my friends, colleagues, professional experts and most importantly other soulful seekers. I let my guard down, quieted the ego, made it okay to be wrong and stopped taking myself so damn seriously. I started to discover and accept powerful things about not only myself but about human nature; about the stories we tell ourselves, our decisions and impulses and the deceitful filters we develop and are so often misguided by. I learned what my intrinsic values were and admittedly what they were not and about the vulnerabilities that have so often tripped me up? It became so simple yet so empowering — *the clearest path to freedom is acceptance.*

This SHIFT helped create circumstances and opened paths that were in alignment with my particular style of energy, my talents and creative sensibilities, my sacred dream space and in support of my truest place of purpose. What wondrously came out of my pain state was great empathy for others. What people felt, and what they were experiencing became much more important. I became so grateful to all of those loving angelic souls who recognized my suffering and cared enough to selflessly listen and offer their wisdom. Perhaps it is because they too had courageously braved the process of "peeling back the layers," and had stepped away from the ego in order to enlighten their own path towards a clearer and deeper understanding of themselves and the broader climate of the world around them. I realized it is when we begin to let go and naturally move to the vibration of our own order, our own collective conscious and dawn of awareness that we can start to live out a more connected, helpful, complete, balanced and positive life journey. Balance, awareness, gratitude and joy lead me into moments of pure delight and helped create and influence an expansive eternal essence and personal awakening.

I was no longer plagued and imprisoned by the disappointed lesser version of myself, but astounded and grateful for my sacred perfection and the value that I contribute to strengthening the oneness of us all. I owe immeasurable appreciation to all of the loving people who have graciously bestowed their precious gifts of eternal wisdom onto me.

Today I take life moment by moment, leaning into resistance, challenging limiting beliefs, continuing gentle self- correction and contently continuing my journey toward a rich and purpose driven life. In an effort to remember my armor of wisdom I created the following list of thoughts that have proved very helpful for me to maintain balance and stay well grounded in astounding clarity:

- Submit and let go of ego
- Come to a place of pure acceptance
- Be truly present, enjoy the art of "mindful being"
- Breathe deeply
- Become as kind to yourself as you are to your friends
- Enlarge your future by forgiving yourself and others

- Continually seek and embrace wisdom as you grow
- Think higher and feel more
- Embrace your perfect imperfections, celebrate the essence of your goodness
- Be grateful and remain open to all that is possible
- And remember to give yourself away to the good of all things

Standing back, viewing things on a more global and selfless level makes all the work and purpose much bigger than us! It is no longer *my* or *your* responsibility to make it all happen and make it all right. The SHIFT allows us to turn our petty judgments and frustrations into gratitude by embracing them as valuable time honored lessons and glorious thoughts and experiences. The matrix dynamically changes by accepting yourself for what and who you are and becomes more simplified by celebrating all that you have. It melts the egotistical perception of ourselves and instead helps us to love ourselves from our most honest place of value. Everything becomes enough, lighter, lifted and open to just *be* – SHIFTING into a calming state of joy.

Stay on course; do not ever stop imagining greatness even if you can only find it in this one magnificent moment. Nothing affirms our lives, dreams or life's work more than experiencing the magic of truly becoming. We never need to wait for something good or magnificent to come into our lives, it is already here — simply SHIFT into and accept the perfectness of you.

About the Author

Deidre Trudeau is the owner and Creative Director of Ezeeye Imaging & ezones.biz, a speaker, author and founder of *The SheFluence Factor — Explore, Tap into, Own and Wildly Expand Your Influence to create a More Positive Impact in Your Life, Business, Community and the World!* & author of *Social SheFluence: Tap into the Powerful SheConomy*, Reach out with effective brand presence that fully engages meaningful connections and Powers Lasting Results! Co-founder of Women's Success Today, and on the executive team for Solutions 4 Life (S4L). Deidre is also an award winning fine artist, talented graphic designer, brand strategist, spirited Innovator and visionary collaborator.

Remember *Good Design Looks Good... But Sells Even Better!*

Get Noticed - Stay Connected!

www.SheFluenceFactor.com
Ezeeye Imaging
http://www.ezeeye.com
http://www.ezones.biz
Phone: 916-803-2787

Are You One of the Living Dead?

Amani Jackson

Your life is over. You are sure of it. How can you recuperate from all of the losses, all of the mistakes? The positive slogans abound but you are numb to them. People have their struggles but not like yours. No one understands what you are experiencing and it is a waste of time to confide in or even speak with anyone about it. STOP IT! This is a negative mentality and all that it will produce is negative energy, negative results and a negative lifestyle. No good will come of it. It is absurd to walk around every day living your life as if it is already over. You have become the living dead! If you are breathing you are in a position to change your circumstance.

I have found myself in the very same situation. Defeated. All I could do was lay in bed awake at night replaying past mistakes in my head and wishing I had made the alternate decision. Why did I get this degree over that one? Why did I say yes to this relationship? Why didn't I leave the relationship when the first warning signal sounded? Why did I get into another relationship that showed the same qualities as the other disastrous ones? Why did I say this, do

Conversations That Make a Difference

that or allow it? I was making myself ill. The voices in my head were so noisy I could not hear anything outside of myself; not even the help my friends and family were trying to offer.

Then I thought of all of the celebrities and millionaires who shared their stories. Tyler Perry had once been homeless, but now is an actor, author, screenwriter, playwright, producer, director and songwriter. J.K. Rowling, author of the *Harry Potter* series, was a single parent depending on welfare to provide for her family. There are countless others who were strung out on drugs, children of abusive or drug addicted parents, high school drop outs and more. However, their perspective allowed them to rise above their circumstance and achieve the lives that they wanted in spite of the obstacles.

After some reflection I came up with a few helpful tips to assist in overcoming these mental impediments. First things first, let's get out of the blame game. You may not have gotten the resources that you needed earlier in life, you didn't get the support that would have helped, you didn't get the love that you deserved and the list goes on. Well, join the club. What you did get was another chance at life when you woke up this morning. Now stop wasting it and make the best out of it. What you must realize is that you have everything that you need inside of you at this very moment, and unleashing your full potential into the world is just one decision away. It's all up to you how far you go on this journey called life. Why drown yourself in the quicksand of negativity and regret when you can opt for the road of positivity and opportunity? That's right, it's a choice.

Take a moment to find yourself. Understand your strengths and weaknesses; accepting them both as a part of

Shift Your Beliefs to Get What You Want

who you are. Then embrace and rejoice in the fact that the weakness does not have to remain a permanent fixture in your life. It can be worked on until it is resolved. Find what your passion is in life and pursue it. Eradicate the people in your life who are not supportive and do not add value. There is no use in burdening yourself with people who will remind you of past mistakes or who will not inspire you to achieve your goals. Do not tolerate others spewing negativity into your life. If you are releasing your negative thoughts and energy why in the world would you entertain theirs? Your magnificence will make the right people gravitate towards you. Be content with the fact that not everyone will be a part of your journey. Don't let their rejection of you cause you to question yourself.

Once you find the path that you want to take, refuse to let doubt and fear take residence within you. There is no reason that someone else is living a great life and you are not. Nothing that they have done is out of your reach. Your drive, your mindset is the transport system that will get you to your desired destination. Do not allow a negative or doubtful thought process to keep the brakes on the train destined for greatness.

While it is true that knowing the right people can open doors for you in life, it is equally true about possessing the right attitude. The law of attraction states that like attracts like. Therefore, not only will having an upbeat outlook attract others with an upbeat outlook, but it will attract success, opportunity and conditions conducive to a happy life, a happy you.

Whenever thoughts enter your mind that are adverse to your well-being, confront them. Remind yourself that you are human. Your mistakes did not break you, they built you. Try not to look at past errors with regret, but instead, as lessons that light your path toward the finish line. If you make another poor decision in life it's alright. We do not strive to make bad decisions but there are lessons in them just the same. We did not graduate from school after just one class did we?

The reality is no one is on this planet by chance. Everyone has a purpose and is necessary. There are far too many people with life saving ideas or inventions that would increase our quality of life, yet they go unintroduced. Often this occurs because people lack focus, guidance or support. That is robbery. Imagine where the world could be with so many of the advances that were never brought to fruition. Let's face it, sometimes we will be the only supporters that we have. Do not rob the world of what you have to offer it.

What plagued me the most beyond my insecurities, doubts and fears was the potential for being unfulfilled. At the end of our lives we will replay our days, opportunities taken and missed. I strive to never have to ask myself 'what if?' Today, I would much rather try yet not succeed, than to never witness what I can accomplish. A fulfilled life, whether it is full of trial and error, misfortune or success, is far better than a life void of the experiences and growth they bring.

So, unless you plan to dig a plot and bury yourself today, it's time to start living on purpose and with purpose. Invest in your dreams, believe in yourself and love the one life that you have. Do everything with zeal and vigor. Every time that you feel as if you can't accomplish a task, that you are not good enough or that you have messed up too many times, brush it off and ask yourself, "Why not me?" The thought that you can't is an absolute falsehood because you can. The fear that you will fail is simply a crutch that allows you to play it safe and never experience the heights to which you can soar. When those moments arise remember Bethany Hamilton, a soul surfer whose loss of an arm did not stop her from living her dream. Keep in mind that Marla Runyan was the first legally blind athlete in the Olympics. Despite her inability to see her path, her vision led the way.

Refrain from playing it safe to decrease the odds of disappointment and failure. Go after your dreams with a fierce determination and passion. Be an inspiration to all of those around you. Be contagious and assist other with climbing out of their graves. Take every opportunity to prove your insecurities wrong. Never surrender. Live, live and live some more until the option is no longer yours.

Conversations That Make a Difference

About the Author

Amani Jackson has had a passion for writing since her elementary years. This passion produced to published children's books and has propelled her to venture into poetry and fiction for both young adults and adults. Born in Newark, N.J., Amani can relate to dreams being stifled by lack of resources and aspires to be instrumental in assisting the youth bridge that gap. She is also the founder of My Sister's Keeper, an organization geared to encourage young girls to maintain their virginity or arrest promiscuous behavior if they have already began. In addition, the organization serves to promote a mentoring, community service and educational emphasis in their lives. When she is not writing, Amani prefers to spend her time travelling.

Please feel free to visit www.amanijackson.com to view her books and events or contact her at authoramanijackson@aol.com

Happy reading!

The Shift from Grief to Grace

Christine Gregory Campos

Beliefs are invisible for the most part. It is said that 50% of a person's belief system is formed by the time they are five years old and just about 100% of their belief system is solid by the age of eighteen. Beliefs affect our lives in every way possible. They create the foundation of every single decision.

When you are in the emotion of grief, you are in the belief that your loved one is dead. While a collective belief about death already exists, within that collective belief is an individual interpretation based on personal experiences and belief systems.

It may sound harsh and crazy to speak of grief in this way, it may even sound borderline insensitive. I promise you these words do not come from a place of judgment nor opinion, but rather from a place in my heart; a place I've found to trust.

In May of 2012 my oldest son died from accidental overdose. I had done absolutely everything I could within my ability, both financially and emotionally, to help him. Since beginning this journey of life without my son, Brendon, I've learned so much about life, death, addiction, intuition and grief. These lessons have brought me from a space of grief to a place of grace.

I was devastated to learn of my son's passing. The general consensus belief is "a child should not pass before a parent." While recently listening to Hay House Radio featuring Terri Daniel and The Afterlife Awareness, Terri said something that touched my heart to be a truth for me. She asked, "Why is it that people think a child should not pass before a parent? What if they had come here with a mission and their mission was complete?" She said that it is because of what and how we've been taught to believe about death that makes it so tragic.

I remember when my daughter was in first grade, one of her classmates had passed from a battle with cancer. That same day, my grandmother also lost her battle with cancer. These deaths did not seem the same to me.

This little girl's parents fought so hard and desperately for her life, just as we had fought for Brendon's life. Regardless, the outcome was the same — passing from this life to what we call death. This leads me to talk about "belief systems" and how they truly impact our daily living.

Consider this analogy to demonstrate the power beliefs hold over our lives: Today, when someone has cancer the conjoint belief is that the person is a victim of the disease. When someone is addicted, people generally believe that it is completely a choice made by the free will of the individual. The real truth is that while trying a drug is a choice — becoming an addict is not. It's truly all in the body's chemistry. Just as being prone to cancer, one is prone to addiction; however, that belief is not common.

Shift Your Beliefs to Get What You Want

Beliefs are not facts but are treated as such. There are combinations of individual beliefs and collective beliefs (i.e. of a society, culture or religion, etc.)

Our belief systems have conditioned us to take a victim mentality approach to cancer. We have been trained and educated to believe that we are powerless. Nothing could be further from the truth. There is ample medical research demonstrating that we can help protect our bodies against cancer getting into cells. D-Limonene, found in natural essential oils, actually protects the membrane of the cell wall preventing the intrusion of cancer into the cell. This factoid is not touted by the medical community or the major broadcast stations. These belief systems about cancer and treatments are built on data from an industry that profits from illness.

Addiction is an illness not only deeply seated in the mind, heart and body, but also in the soul (spirit) of a person. There is tons of medical research indicating that addiction needs to be treated as a multifaceted disease — yet we continue to treat addicts as criminals, we continue to prosecute those who are trapped in addiction.

My point is that we are trained to believe that there are only specific medically approved protocols that can help a person who has cancer, and that cancer carries a life or death sentence. Similarly, we have the same belief system when it comes to treating addiction. I also contend that we have similarly existing taught-belief systems when it comes to the topic of death.

When my son passed, I did not allow myself the choice to be immobilized by grief. I pushed myself to move when every part of my body wanted to die. After all, it was my belief that no parent should ever lose a child.

Conversations That Make a Difference

When I think about that belief itself, "no parent should ever lose a child," it is a very a defining thought process. It sets the boundaries of how I can think or what I can feel. Learning to question that belief has helped me change my experience with grief.

Other beliefs I learned to challenge include what happens when someone dies. Are we simply humans in physical bodies and once we pass we cease to be? Can our loved ones still see us and communicate with us? Are our loved ones punished in some way for not meeting some earthly standard? I've learned to question several of the things that I thought to be true about death. I've learned that much of my belief system is truly based on what I was taught and not what I have learned myself. Shifting a belief can change perspective on your life from the dark of night to the light of day.

In my desperate need to make some sense of my son's death, I began to explore the disease of addiction and poured myself into reading, learning and understanding all I could about this life-crippling disease. I knew my son was very ill and yet I was at a complete and utter loss of how to help him. Popular opinion was that he was doing this to himself, and he should just suck it up and have some character and just get over it. But what if those beliefs are not accurate? What if those beliefs were built on a false sense of beliefs or inaccurate or undiscovered information?

I remember being in an interview with a gentleman who said, "People will not question what they believe. They will never go back and look at history to uncover what they may not know." That is a recipe for building inaccurate beliefs. I hope this inspires you to consider taking back your power, and as my son said, "Think for yourself."

Shift Your Beliefs to Get What You Want

In my quest to help find better answers to treating addiction, I've learned so much more than I ever imagined. I have said and done things since my son's passing that I would never have imagined or thought to do. I have often felt my son is dancing — wherever his spirit continues — to see that I finally understand much of what he tried to tell me while he was in the physical form. I was recently listening to James Van Praagh on Hay House Radio and he said, "Don't look at them as dead." What empowerment that statement has provided me.

I have chosen to share my story in the hope it helps bridge the gap of belief and move from grief to grace. I've learned to be open to new lessons and ideas. I've learned that while things may not make sense from my mental belief system, when I "shift" into my heart center, I am very clear in the inner space of intuitive guidance.

Everyone has the intuitive gene. We've been taught by our belief systems that this is not the truth. We've been taught that this is an extra special gift. I've come to learn that is not true. Just like one has to develop any other skill such as reading, writing, singing or dancing, learning to tap into your intuitive guidance system is just beyond the belief that you can or cannot. If you believe you can, then it is so. Whatever you believe you can achieve is already done.

I've tapped into my heart space. I've been taught by Spirit and intuitive guidance that looking back to the day Brendon passed from physical form back to his natural state of Spirit is only re-traumatizing myself. It serves no one, especially me, to continue to rehash and relive that event. It only takes me from the present moment and keeps me stuck in yesterday's events. What happened is done. No amount of

Conversations That Make a Difference

rehashing it will ever change it. So I've asked myself, what is my lesson? What can I do to help my heart move forward?

Instead of investing my time into yesterday, I've decided to be open to what my lessons are in this lifetime. To understand and believe in my heart that Brendon finished his lessons brings me some peace of mind. I believe his spirit continues. I believe he stands just beyond the shadows of the veil, always there beside me.

One of my mentors taught me that our language around death is so important. I haven't really "lost" Brendon, I just lost the ways I was "used to" communicating with him. By going into my heart space and quieting my mind, I've found peace in learning new ways to connect with him. It is through developing the confidence in my intuition that I have found this peace. The more I retreat inwardly and depend upon my heart's intuitive guidance, the more peace I find. This intuitive guidance opens doors I never imagined. I've surrendered to simply what is and make no mental conclusion on it.

I am not saying that you should never feel sad. We live in the world of duality. Our beliefs are based on duality. What I am suggesting is do not get stuck in the sadness; find the space in your heart that can bring you out of it. What if everything really is in divine synchronicity? I encourage you to brave and embrace the sadness. Crying helps release the trauma from within you. Grief is a one-day-at-a-time process; some days will be easier than others. If you feel overwhelmed by your sadness, retreat within. Pick up your journal and write. Write the thoughts from your mind and then listen to the answers from your heart. Question the beliefs behind the thoughts that are creating your reality for today. Ask for guidance of finding new ways to celebrate the one you love. Choose your words so that they empower you.

It is my wish that if you are experiencing grief in your life, find your intuitive guidance system. It is there waiting for you to find it. If you hear a small voice in your mind, trust it. If you have a feeling in your gut, feel it and trust it. It may be dreams or flashes of ideas in your mind's eye, or it may just be a strong sense of knowing — a knowing that goes beyond truths or beliefs you've learned; trust them. Decide to adopt the mindset to not look at your loved one as "dead," because in truth that is only perhaps what you've been taught to believe and as Terri Daniel said, "The way we perceive death is a choice."

About the Author

Christine Gregory Campos, has dedicated her life to follow Divine Guidance and has been blessed with the ability to communicate with the Angels. She is a Certified Angel Therapist, Certified Angel Card Reader and an Intuitive Business Marketing Strategist. She lives in Tampa, Florida with her son Ryan. Her daughter Brianna, has returned to college for her Master's Degree in Counseling. Christine is the Founder and Creator of The Brendon Project, a Project of Love. She has joined with the energy of many other organizations working to change the "face" of addiction and find better answers to addiction treatment. To find out more about Christine visit
www.about.me/ChristineGregoryCampos
Christine's email addresses:
christine@thebrendonproject.com
christine@marketingintentionally.com

Your Best You: *Unleashed!!!*

Deborah Respress

Seriously ... Is this how it ALL ends? ... Am I really going to DIE RIGHT NOW?" I fearfully thought in my mind, while my mouth desperately asked questions, over and over again, to an unseen Divine Presence I called GOD.

"What about all the things I am suppose to do? ... What about my kids? ... Is this really happening NOW? ... Are YOU kidding me?" I angrily pleaded in disbelief, as the realization had become clear to me, GOD was not joking ... this was FOR REAL!

For too long, I had ignored all of the warning signs. I was always the strong one that everyone else came to and leaned upon. I was expected to give them strength, guidance, and support during their trials and tribulations on this journey we called LIFE. I was more than willing and happy to oblige them! Before they could finish saying, "Help Me ... Rescue Me," I had already dusted off my Earth Angel wings, put on my Superwoman tights, leaped upon my metaphysical white horse or black stallion, whichever best suited my mood or energy, and galloped off to "Save Their Day!" During all of my "SHE-roics" and "The Adventures of Deborah," I had forgotten something very, very important. I had neglected to also take care of ME!

And then, IT happened! *BAM ... Lights Out!* Something short-circuited. My head felt dizzy, my heart became heavy, my body collapsed, and I was unable to move. I knew that I was in trouble. What was even worse, I was HOME ALONE ... IN TROUBLE!

"Okay GOD, I get the message ... I need to slow down a little ... I get it," was my initial reaction. I had overexerted myself in the past and sometimes taken on a little more than I should, one way or another. But, I was always able to count upon some type of "Divine or Angelic Intervention" on my behalf. However, this time, things were very different. My attempted effort to "talk myself out of this one," like some type of "Prodigal Daughter" who wanted to go back home, was not working. This time, I knew I had gone too far!

"Please GOD ... don't let me become one of those people who DIE with their music still inside of them." I quietly pleaded. But GOD appeared unimpressed and only responded with the "Silent" SILENCE! This was not good. I had lived long enough to discern the difference between, "The SILENCE," which <u>was</u> a good thing for me, and "The Silent SILENCE," which <u>was not</u> a good thing for me.

In "The SILENCE," I could always use the higher vibrational levels of my five senses to see, feel, hear, smell and/or touch my way into GOD'S PRESENCE and this would give me great comfort, peace, vision and guidance. But, on the other hand, in "The Silent SILENCE" it seemed as if all of my connections were blocked and I could not easily sense The Divine Presence. This caused much fear, doubt and unbelief to set in, joined with anxiety and stress, which made everything very noisy inside of me.

Shift Your Beliefs to Get What You Want

Desperately and angrily I pleaded in disbelief at GOD'S Silent SILENCE. *"Seriously ... Is this how it ALL ends? ... Am I really going to DIE RIGHT NOW?"* But, I could not hear, see or feel GOD. Slowly and sadly, I reconciled my shocked mind to the reality of the situation ... "There will be No Divine Intervention ... TONIGHT!" I said. And, then suddenly, out of nowhere, *BOOM!* My body, unable to stabilize itself any longer, TOTALLY BLACKED OUT!!!

While my body was "Blacked Out," I had a very, very strange, surreal and mystical dream. I could see my body, motionless and unresponsive, collapsed on my bed. I felt the beating of my heart, and the awareness of my mind and soul all pulsating deep from within. I could hear the voice of my spirit, enfolded in and through my body. As I followed the voice of my spirit, I envisioned brilliant beams of light extended from me, both upward and inward to a higher plane.

I soon felt "THE DREAM" within my dream. I saw a bridge of energy and light leading to a realm of higher forces, populated by a diverse group of celestial hosts, angel guardians, spiritual guides and other higher beings. As they encircled me, I could sense the Divine Presence of GOD, moving towards me. It felt as if I was being carefully examined by "All-That-Is." Every thought of my mind, every cell of my body, every longing of my heart, every code of my soul and every purpose of my spirit, were being discerned by The Presence, and discussed amongst the group. Eventually, I realized that they were in the process of determining whether or not I would be given more time in this body!

They continued to talk amongst themselves, about me, as if I was not there! Eventually, I could no longer contain myself. "What about all the things I am suppose to do? ...

Conversations That Make a Difference

What about my kids? ... Is this really happening NOW? ... Are YOU kidding me?" I desperately blurted out to them. But, it appeared as if they did not hear me. "Please give me another chance! ... I promise that I will become the person that 'I AM' yet to become! ... I will take better care of myself ... Please guide me and show me what I need to do!" I quietly pleaded directly to the Divine Presence. Suddenly, there was "The SILENCE." And I once again felt comforted and peaceful. I visualized a cord of light coming out of my belly button area that linked me with the source of ALL life. And then ... "THE DREAM" within my dream ended.

The next morning, I awakened to the most beautiful sunlight streaming through my bedroom window. "Thank You GOD, Thank You GOD, Thank You GOD!" I shouted out loud. "Thank You for giving me another day! Thank You for allowing me to be, what You created me to be ... and do what You created me to do! Thank You for giving me more time with my children, my family, my friends ... and to make a positive difference in the world! Thank You! Thank You! Thank You!" I continued, deeply and sincerely grateful for the second chance, GOD had given me, in this thing called LIFE! This "One-Woman," heartfelt praise and worship celebration was interrupted when I eventually heard my cell phone ringing.

It was my dear friend, Charles, calling to check in on me. Charles and I had established a beautiful habit of touching basis with one another each morning. We would lovingly wish each other the most powerful, wonderful and fantastic days. But, on that morning things were very different. "What's wrong?" Charles asked, as he detected a different tone in my voice. Slowly, I told him about everything that happened the night before to my body, and about some of

Shift Your Beliefs to Get What You Want

the details I remembered from my strange dreams. Abruptly, Charles interrupted me, and quickly stated, in a "NO NONSENSE" manner, "We are going to the hospital ... I'm taking you to the emergency room!" He said. "But I don't have any insurance." I said. "We will figure it out! ... I will make a few phone calls to find some options for you ... while you get ready to go ... I will see you soon!" Charles insisted, and ended the call before I could attempt to convince him otherwise.

When we arrived at the hospital emergency room, I was in for a major surprise ... THEY KEPT ME!! The doctors and technicians ran several tests on me. The results were "abnormal," and my body could not be stabilized. Eventually, one of the emergency room doctors informed me that I needed to be admitted into the hospital to be further tested and monitored by a specialist until they figured out what was going on with my body. Reluctantly, I agreed to stay. By this time, the morning had turned into night. Sadly, I told Charles, "I will not be going home tonight!" He calmly responded, "I'm very sorry to hear that, but I think it's a good thing that you came to the hospital!" Quietly, I agreed, and thanked Charles for his support. Soon, my body and mind felt very drowsy, from the medicines administered to me by the nurse. "You should go home and get some rest." I said to Charles. "I'll see you in Dreamland!" I playfully added, before he left.

Over the next 24 hours, the doctors were finally able to stabilize my systems. After being satisfied with the results of a battery of tests they ran on me, they were able to prescribe the right combination of medicines that worked for my body. Later that evening, I was cleared to go home, with many instructions from them on ways to take better care of myself. Just then, my younger sister, Barbara, appeared and offered to drive me home.

Conversations That Make a Difference

When I returned home, I recalled and reflected upon the events of the past 72 hours, that I had experienced. I remembered my body collapsing, "THE DREAM," within my dream, and all of the events that led up to my hospitalization. While I was grateful that the doctors had stabilized my physical body, and addressed the effects of whatever was going on with me, I wasn't fully satisfied. I wanted to know more about the underlying spiritual or metaphysical causes of my body's traumatized physical effects as well. Soon I quieted myself within, stilled my mind and asked The Divine Presence of GOD, to show me the answer.

After a few moments, "The SILENCE" revealed the *LAW OF YOUR BEST YOU* to me!

The *LAW OF YOUR BEST YOU* is based upon the powerful, timeless and often forgotten ancient law of the scriptures, which states, *"If you bring forth what is within you, what you bring forth will save you. If you do not bring forth what is within you, what you do not bring forth will destroy you!"*

The *LAW OF YOUR BEST YOU* is a set of expanded beliefs upon the ancient scriptural law, that held, *"You are both Human and Divine, a Spiritual Being in a Human Body. Your Divine, Spiritual Self, which is created in the 'Image and Likeness of GOD,' is your Authentic Self ... 'YOUR BEST YOU!'"*

This revelation *of the LAW OF YOUR BEST YOU*, led to a very dynamic, pivotal and transformational "a-ha moment" and "paradigm shift" within my overall consciousness!

Somewhere along the way, while I was trying to save and rescue everyone else, I had forgotten to *bring forth what was within me to save ME!* My *BEST YOU*, had become neglected, tangled and bound ... and this was destroying me! It was at this point that I realized what I had to do. My *BEST YOU* had to be UNLEASHED!

Shift Your Beliefs to Get What You Want

With *YOUR BEST YOU: UNLEASHED,* my journey of empowerment continued, and has led me to serve and empower others to **Become, Create and Live the Life of YOUR BEST YOU!**

Guidance and Suggestions to UNLEASH YOUR BEST YOU!

- **Honor Your Soul & Spirit:** Meditate and Pray Every Day! Link Up Your Spirit Daily!
- **Honor Your Mind:** Think About What You Desire, and Not About What You Fear!
- **Honor Your Heart:** Follow Your Highest Joy! Love, Love, Love! Laugh and Play!
- **Honor Your Body:** Sleep 7-8+ Hours Every Night! Rest, Restore & Rejuvenate!
- **Honor Your Purpose:** Energize & Express Your Unique Talents to Serve Humanity!
- **Honor YOUR BEST YOU: *UNLEASHED!***

About the Author

Deborah Respress is driven by a vision to show you how to tap into your inner power, bring forth YOUR BEST YOU, and fulfill your unique purpose. She provides multiplatform communication and empowerment programs, services, and products to help you live an empowered life, grow your business, and serve others with **Your Best You!**

As Founder of Your Best You International, Speaker, Writer, Trainer, Transformational Coach, Actor-Singer-Songwriter, and Executive Producer of the *Blue Rose at Midnight* music CD, Deborah empowers and entertains, as she educates. Utilizing the *LAW OF YOUR BEST YOU,* she combines transformational energy and manifestation principles with practical strategies to help you bring your life up to the level of your highest vision!

Become, Create, and Live the Life of YOUR BEST YOU!

Learn more about Deborah at:
www.DeborahRespress.com and
www.YourBestYou.com
Get your copy of her *Blue Rose at Midnight CD* at:
www.cdbaby.com/EarthAngelMusic
Contact her at:
deborah@DeborahRespress.com

Shift Your Beliefs to Get What You Want

Cooking For Personal Transformation

Rachael J. Avery

A veggie Mexican casserole dish saved my life. To gain deep personal insight, people may watch Super Soul Sunday, Dr. Phil, or pick up the latest Wayne Dyer book. For me, divine introspection arrives in the form of dinner. Cooking is my life teacher; dinner is my daily lesson. It's hard to believe one dinner can change your life.

Six years ago, I had a spiritual awakening in the kitchen and have been cooking in a different light ever since. I've gently learned how to whip up a vibrant, playful, colorful life to include morning chai green tea while bobbing in the pool on a Tuesday morning in Florida. I exchanged alarm clocks for inspiration, a scale for serenity, calories for creativity, and vowed to never use the three letter "f" word again. Even though my weight fluctuates, I love and honor myself. I adjust my wardrobe to comfort instead of what size I should be in. A little work gets folded into play and purposeful projects. Cardinals perch everyday on the fence to offer me truths in how the universe is rooting for my magical happiness.

However, my life wasn't always so fresh and zesty bobbing in the pool.

Six years ago, I answered the question, "What's for dinner? There's nothing to eat!" with Taco Bell #3 extra red sauce and a diet Dr. Pepper. Unless it was ideal conditions, I dreaded cooking. I thought meal time — especially dinner — was the most persistent, nagging reminder that my life was too hectic, too busy, and too crazy to stop and make a nourishing meal.

They way I felt about cooking and food mirrored how I felt about my life.

I was 60 lbs. overweight, had a negative bank account, a foreclosure on my home, an abusive relationship defined me, had just received my second job layoff, and a severe bipolar manic depressive episode lay me on the couch for three months. Hope had officially left the building.

I decided there was no way out except to take my own life. As life escaped my body, a powerful inner voice I'd never heard before said with thunder, "GET UP! GET UP! GET UP! I am not done with you yet."

Hearing a higher inner voice with such velocity for the first time terrified me. I awakened and stood up, bandaging my own wounds, and stumbling down the hall.

"Where do you want me to go?" I screamed from the pit of my stomach. "I have nowhere to go and nothing to live for!"

Before I could be any more confused, the once forceful higher voice fell soft and gentle. I found my two feet planted in my kitchen. I had an empty pantry, fridge, and was drained of life; yet the now gentle voice whispered, "I want you to create something from nothing, my dear."

Shift Your Beliefs to Get What You Want

What came of my culinary spiritual awakening was a veggie Mexican casserole dish that to this day I have yet to recreate. Up until that point in my life, I never created something so beautiful, nourishing, and authentic from such little resources. I had never been so seamlessly inspired without effort when at the lowest point in my life. My level of creativity, talent and power could not be explained, but would be with me in the kitchen ever since.

Do you sometimes feel stale, immobilized, like you're hitting a brick wall in any one area of your life? Do you feel helpless that your situation is different and unique because nothing has ever worked permanently? Do you feel like having to start all over again? Or do you feel abundant, loved, and radiate light but you want to deepen your gift to the world beyond your dreams?

As human light beings with a unique gift to give, channels are easily blocked by chocolate and diet coke. We don't know where to start when we need to change something galactic about our lives so we buy Doritos and dip indecision into ranch dip. Heck, often we don't even know what to make for dinner so we order pizza and wings. The next day we get an unsettling, ungrounded feeling from regret, we don't know where to start and subconsciously give up. That is why we feel we need to start over again. If ever you don't know where to start consider the fact that

Your kitchen, cooking, and your relationship with food is your most accessible and affordable place to start personal transformation 24/7.

Your power comes from your ability to harness confidence in small everyday living spaces. There are no road blocks, auditions, or bad cooks in the kitchen. Showing up in willingness is 90% of cooking. Every successful meal is your star dust treasure. Every cooking disaster is your teacher. Cooking is your grace. Divine grace has been set before you at least 3 times a day in such simple forms you've forgotten how powerful it is. You're already standing in your solution when you stand in the kitchen. Your two feet planted in the kitchen is enough to absorb forgiveness in your soul and begin flinging cilantro in creative spirits. You have just found you. Your power. Your power grows with practice. You can take your new found culinary ninja powers and take it to the streets. You can begin to fold and blend creativity, self-forgiveness, bravery into your job, your career, to dance with your purpose.

Inspired nourishing meals are THE key foundation to an inspired nourishing life.

Imagine how your life would be different if you were confident and creative with cooking and knew every single night that you had dinner at home waiting to nourish you? Would you be free to spend time with your family, take up a dance lesson, or take a meditative bath?

You have a fierce hot jalapeño purpose to do in this world. If you don't know where to start or feel like there is a road block in your life hop in the kitchen and use the most basic five life lessons to help you. Every time you begin to start changing some aspect of your life and you're not sure where to begin; start with dinner. Start forgiving yourself for everything you put in your mouth, for everything you cook, every which way you cook it. Try new things to stay creative and inspired, use what you already have to stay grateful, turn on the music and play, and empty yourself of every rotting moldy thought in your head that is no longer serving your mission.

Shift Your Beliefs to Get What You Want

If you feel your life shift is as far away as dancing on the moon over my hammy, I encourage you to shift your perspective about a quarter cup next time you're cooking by trying something you've never tried before. Learn how to cut a cumquat.

Simply turning into the frequency and intent that cooking is a self-learning platform is all you need to convert your kitchen into an episode as powerful as Super Soul Sunday.

Consider being an open channel to absorb these life lessons next time you're in the kitchen to make the next meal time heal time for your soul.

5 BIGGEST LIFE LESSONS TO LEARN FROM COOKING

FORGIVENESS - Celebrate your next mistake in the kitchen! Next time you burn garlic gluten free bread with earth balance butter say, "Who wants Cajon croutons? They're as perfect as am I!" Practicing the art of self-forgiveness in the kitchen and celebrating mistakes rids your life of guilt and shame.

CREATIVITY COUNTS - Try new things! See ingredients you already have in different ways. Can you use a collard green leaf as a tortilla? Consider using your favorite organic jam as a sweetener to your own oil and vinegar dressing. Cook with the colors of the chakras to balance energy centers. When we see what we have differently, with creativity, our resources expand exponentially.

GET GRATEFUL - Do you really think the garlic powder now hard as a rock from five years ago lingering in the corner of your spice pantry is serving you? Clear the energy and increase vibrational flow by releasing what you no longer use. Clear your pantry as you cook. As you gain clarity you become grateful.

PLAY - Is there a reason why you're uptight in the kitchen? Release your clenched buttocks long enough to play some music, light a candle, and practice some of those Dancing With the Stars moves in the kitchen. Try Cook-aroke to spice up the atmosphere. Use playfulness to overcome tired don't feel like cooking bad mood blues.

EMPTY YOURSELF - The fridge isn't the only thing in need of a good cleaning. Empty your head and your heart before walking into the kitchen. Ask your guides to help empty limiting dinner beliefs. When you empty yourself, you leave space for your Higher Inner Chef to come in.

It was cooking for personal transformation that turned the worst day of my life into my sprout of personal power. Only after months of building my intuitive culinary confidence, I miraculously seeped forgiveness into my heart. With forgiveness, I began the journey of blessing and releasing 60 lbs. from my physical body.

- I used creativity to see what I had differently and to leave a thirteen year abusive relationship.
- I got grateful by looking at my circumstances differently. I began to see powerful resources and started my own business.
- I used my playful spirit to release depression medications from my life and found joy.

Shift Your Beliefs to Get What You Want

- I fearlessly emptied my mind and trusted my Higher Inner Chef to do what I could not do for myself.

Cooking and our relationship to food is the core foundation in our happiness. None of us can avoid interacting with food. We all must eat. Use divine culinary opportunity to learn something about yourself. Become an awakened cook not only because it enhances your life, become an awakened cook because it changes how you feel about your life.

Dinner is not just dinner. Dinner is your daily life lesson placed here as an opportunity to expand yourself.

If you've already made giant life shifts and are currently marinating in abundance like myself — cooking through personal transformation will brûlée your dreams even further and strengthen your manifestation, business creativity, vitality, health and bliss.

Start with dinner tonight. To begin working with your Highest Inner Chef I offer this simple affirmation, *I am open to cooking with my Highest Inner Chef.*

If you are already masterful in the kitchen, infuse the flavor of your current practice with this affirmation, *Surprise me, Highest Inner Chef!*

Life can distract us from our purpose. Job losses, weight gain, and home foreclosure can easily bring us to our knees — tripping us into buckets of chocolate faster than you can say Willy Wonka. Excuses prevail as to why the next step on our juicy little journey is unattainable. Next time you feel overwhelmed, uninspired, or a road block is keeping you from your light, consider hopping in the kitchen and being an open channel of nourishment. You don't need all of the measurements, all of the tricks, or have the gadgets. After all, life often doesn't give us the recipe.

Conversations That Make a Difference

All you need is four ingredients for dinner relief tonight. After using your affirmation simply ponder what you have in your own kitchen right now in the following categories:

PROTEIN - do you have chicken, beef, lentils, black beans, tofu?

STARCH - do you have potatoes, brown rice, flax bread?

VEGETABLE - do you have broccoli, carrots, kale?

COLOR - incorporate as many different colors on your plate as possible.

Feel free to use this simple concept for your grocery list too. This is my very basic intuitive meal planning I use for all my workshops using ten cooking concepts.

Never underestimate the power of a small, affordable, practical place in your home like a kitchen to transform your life.

I like to think that people are like spices; we each have our own unique flavor, healing properties, and purpose. Although each of us is tasty on our own, our true potency and yumminess happens when we marinate together and enhance the flavor of each other's gifts. When we do that, magic happens.

To keep your personal transformation journey rich and saucy I have only one question for you, "What's for dinner? There's nothing to eat."

About the Author

Rachael J. Avery is a Certified Food and Spirit Practitioner, awakening audiences to the power and joy of cooking. She teaches Intuitive Meal Planning Workshops and Chakra Food Healing in Tampa, FL. Most recently, Rachael J. launched a Cooking with Kids Club; a plant based, sugar free, gluten free cooking community.

She is the author of, *30 Day Social Media Detox* and a children's books series, *Netty Noo and Her Friends, Too*, helping children to find friends in nature. Rachael J. owns The Grateful Pantry, an on-line community of people she calls grateful go getters, interested in learning more about the unique freedom in concept cooking, intuitive cooking, and alternatives to cookbook and recipe thinking.

She volunteers as Toastmasters Youth Leadership Chair for the Tampa Bay Area bringing speaking and leadership skills to high school youth. Rachael J. is a kitten foster parent for a local animal rescue agency.

Connect with her www.thegratefulpantry.com

The Ultimate Power of Changing Your Beliefs!

Dame DC Cordova

How does someone move from being filled with fear, sadness and loss to being a CEO of an organization and teacher of transformational programs designed to teach people to become wealthy and able to have a positive impact in their spheres of influence? I can think of so many examples of how shifting my beliefs have ultimately allowed me to live the life of my dreams since my late twenties. During my late teen years and through my mid-twenties, my life was filled with fear, sadness and loss. Once I began to learn what are called "Mastery Principles," my life changed for the better — forever. This shift in belief has allowed me to tackle some very tough situations, many in business.

To give you a little overview, I have a profound understanding that ultimately the Spirit within each human being in this world is the "light;" the "generator" of the power that goes through the "filters/lenses" (beliefs) that *always*, not sometimes *always*, shape our experiences.

So why do some people who have this understanding still struggle with not having what they want? Where do those

Shift Your Beliefs to Get What You Want

blocks come from? Mostly, from our subconscious mind, although life itself brings us circumstances that are so overwhelming that the only thing we can do is shift our consciousness to be able to feel some semblance of control. I'm sure you've experienced this at some point in your life.

Beliefs shape our *Mindset/Attitudes* which create our *Behaviors* which create *Results*!

This is true for both personal growth as well as business growth.

Let me give you an example of something that I am experiencing right now.

R. Buckminster Fuller (Bucky) made fifty predictions nearly eighty years ago and they have all come true except for his last one. He predicted that if you were under the age of 40 by 1970 and didn't smoke, your life expectancy would be 140 years. Yes, you read right... 140 years! I believe that this prediction will come true. The fact that all but this one prediction has come true is a pretty powerful statistic.

When I heard Bucky speak of that last prediction while I was in my late twenties I knew it was my responsibility to take care of my health and body if I were going to adopt that belief and not buy into the general agreement that we are destined to die in our '80's; if lucky '90's and anything above that is a major exception. I am happily embracing my age.

Bucky made predictions based on mathematical calculations and by studying nature. He created his own mathematics, "Synergetics" and coined the word "synergy," and was listed in *Time Magazine* as one of the top 100 influencers of the 20th century.

Through Bucky's teachings, we learned about generalized principles, which *always* occur, not sometimes but *always*. Gravity is a generalized principle, as is leverage, and one of our favorites that he taught us: Precession, the mathematical explanation of ripple effects.

He also taught us that science and technology were going to accelerate medical and scientific research because of epidemics like AIDS. This research would find cures that would greatly improve the curing of some diseases like cancer, as well as the longevity of human beings. Bucky passed away on July 1, 1983 so he didn't get to see that he was right; many would live through what was once considered a death sentence.

I choose to believe that I have the ability to keep my body and mind filled with vitality and energy; youthful energy. I believe that every cell in my body responds to how I take care of it. When I moisturize my body every day, I say affirmations and focus on sending good thoughts to every organ, my lymphatic system, and every part of me. I breathe deeply to keep my body oxygenated and vitalized. I do my best to keep it nourished with good food, water, supplements and light exercise. This conscious action keeps me on the path of wellness and longevity.

I see so many people who are already feeling badly about themselves and their age by the time they turn 40, let alone 60 and 70. By then, some believe that their remaining years are limited. Some choose to believe that they don't want to live in an "old and decrepit body," so they might as well die at a "reasonable age." Others act like they are already dying, so they overindulge in habits that will cut their lives short: smoking, drinking and eating unhealthily. They don't do the necessary disciplines to keep their health and energy at a level that can keep their minds and body full of vitality, vigor and enthusiasm while living life to the fullest. In other words, it becomes a self-fulfilling prophecy.

Even worse, they buy into other people's beliefs which agree with and sustain the reality they have created. These people find proof and agreement with their thinking from literature, doctors, prescription medicine ads, negative news and the internet which has articles on just about any point of view.

Many people focus on how old they are getting and keep reinforcing it by saying they "hate their age" and they keep getting older, miserably.

The question becomes, "How can we transform those thoughts and slow down the process of aging?"

Here are a few suggestions:
- Accept where you are in life, no matter your age.
- Relax into whatever situation you are facing, especially if there is nothing you can do to change it.
- If you want to change something, change your beliefs and things will begin to change.

I invite you make your own shift on a daily basis using this insight: When you hear something that is disempowering, no matter who is saying it or how much of an expert they claim to be, if it's not congruent with what you wish to believe, say: "cancel, cancel!" You don't have to say it out loud, but definitely say it in your mind.

What you focus on expands; so what are you choosing to believe and focus on?

Are you still focusing on being how you have always been that hasn't worked for you? Or are you choosing to embrace a new you? Are you *willing* to let go of that which doesn't work for you?

Earlier I was giving you an example of a current situation that I am mastering: staying youthful, vibrant and full of energy. What is your situation, condition or belief that you wish to change?

What's so extraordinary is that beliefs then turn into actions that then become results and then experience acquiring evidence that we can rely on. In turn, we become more and more comfortable with this generalized principle.

Here's another great belief: the more you believe in and love yourself and the more you embrace yourself as you are; the more the universe will support that belief.

There are many things that you do right. It is also likely there are things that you want to change. I recommend that you take an inventory of your beliefs in EVERY area of your life that you desire change.

For example, I am constantly asked how one can be more financially successful; how to reach financial independence – my answer always includes these questions:

- What do you believe about success? Money? Prosperity? Finances?
- What is your "deservability" level?
- Is your consciousness founded on a basic belief that will support you in having prosperity and abundance of money? Resources?

I highly recommend looking for YOUR, YOUR PARENT'S, and YOUR FAMILY'S money beliefs; and if they are not empowering and supporting you to having the life you desire, change them immediately. Do the same with health, career, work, business and your overall well being.

When it comes to money, finances and success, a shift from believing in scarcity to believing in sufficiency will ultimately create abundance and prosperity! Believe me, I have seen this happen all over the world for nearly forty years!

You *can* have only empowering beliefs; yes you *can* and one of the most important beliefs to have is this: the key to your happiness is only a thought away.

Change your mind, change your beliefs and your life will change!

I know that many of the wonderful contributors to this book have taken you on different pathways which may include how to handle, clear and empower yourself with the appropriate beliefs for you. I personally want to speak to that part of you that is so wise, that is so brilliant, that internal GPS that knows just the right places to take you. Choose right now to have the most empowering beliefs about yourself, your life, your money/finances, business, your health, your joy and happiness as well as your ability to contribute to others.

Let's release all those disempowering beliefs you've had about yourself, about your abilities and the support that you may not have received from your beloveds, family, environment and the world. Let's get you focused on what really matters –and create a powerful belief that will be your "center." Try this:

Conversations That Make a Difference

"I am an unlimited human being. I cannot be defined by anything that has happened to me or by any of my negative circumstances. I am now aware, clear and I can manifest the life of my dreams..."

See what happens. You can create any version that works for you — your own creative juices will start manifesting "postulates" that will direct your consciousness daily to having more and more. Direct your life to that which has been divinely created and has the elements that make your heart sing.

Believe that you have the wisdom, the power, the energy and the resources to create the life that you want, and you will always do it with integrity and for the good of all concerned. You will no longer take one step or one action that will hurt yourself or others. Believe that you can do that, and it will happen. You will be taken to places that you couldn't have imagined!

Through this process, as your soul evolves, your body and mind will follow. You will create precessional effects (ripple effects) beyond your dreams; you will also be one of many who are supporting the creation of a world that works for everyone.

When I was twenty-seven years old, I made the commitment that if needed, I'd single-handedly eradicate poverty and hunger in my lifetime. Thank God there are millions who are doing the same. After decades of doing work that "churns out" many social entrepreneurs and having supported many foundations and organizations that are also working on that task, I allow myself to take some credit that the number of people, mostly children, who starve and die from easily curable diseases has dropped to a third!

Shift Your Beliefs to Get What You Want

Although there's still a long way to go, we are heading in the right direction. Why? Because I believe I can do it! Thus, I attract others who believe it, too. Your empowering beliefs will not only affect your life, they will affect others and the whole of humanity.

Yes, you are that powerful!

So what are *you* ready to believe? Take a deep breath and allow yourself to feel the core of your being. You are on the most wonderful journey of your life; the shifting of your beliefs and having the experience, moment to moment, that you have the power to affect the quality of your life and that of others'.

The creators of this book have chosen some amazing masters to support you with powerful distinctions on shifting your beliefs and living the life you want. Now, make sure that you put into practice the recommendations and information that we are sharing. In doing so, the chance that your life will be *sweet* has been multiplied many times.

Wishing you tremendous success! Ho'oponopono...

About the Author

Dame DC Cordova is CEO of Excellerated Business Schools® a global organization with over 100,000 grads from Asia Pacific & North America in English and Chinese. Dame DC Cordova's program Money & You® has inspired some of today's greatest wealth and business experts.

Her purpose: To uplift humanity's consciousness through socially-responsible business.

A philanthropist and humanitarian, DC is known as an Ambassador of New Education with a tireless pursuit to transform educational systems around the world and eradicate poverty and hunger.

DC Cordova is a founding member of the Transformational Leadership Council (TLC), and Southern California Association of Transformational Leaders (ATL); a facilitator for the Pachamama Alliance Symposium; council member of Women Speakers' Association; international business development advisor for SuperLab, The California Women's Conference, the WIN on Line organization; and supports numerous nonprofits.

She is the author of *Money Making Systems*; has co-authored many books, participated in motivational films and TV and is founder of Women, Cash & Divine Matters.

Be the Life

Melodee Meyer

I remember my very first diet. I was twelve. I wasn't overweight. In fact, I was a little underweight. I had always been very tall for my age and skinny as a rail, but the idea of dieting made sense to me. After all, my mom was on a diet and she was everything I wanted to be and everything I believed I would be.

Up until then, I had never thought of my mom as fat. She was just 'Mom', a loving homemaker, who cared for her four kids and hardworking husband. To me, she was beautiful and perfect, but the more she dieted and struggled with her weight, the more I became aware of her concerns. Yes, she had hips and thighs and arms and a belly — all of which were, apparently, too big to be acceptable. Perhaps I was too big to be acceptable too?

My mom diligently followed her eating plan and I tried to follow as best I could. She lost weight and, I found it. By the time I was in high school, my hips were big; my butt was big and big was bad. The more I obsessed about being big, the bigger I got. Thus began a thirty year struggle with weight and food and self. My mother's fault? Ha! I wish it were that simple. My mom had done everything she could. She wanted to protect me from her personal struggles and of course, had no intention of passing them on to me. She had beliefs about her body and her weight that I chose to take on as my own. And as I grew into a woman, I believed being overweight was in my DNA and the struggle with my unfortunate genetics was my destiny.

I was right. My body was a direct reflection of my belief and I gave this belief a lot of power. I believed that I was destined to be fat and so I was.

I never considered changing this belief because I didn't know I could. And even if I did, I wouldn't have known it would make any difference. No one told me that some people believe that they are destined to be healthy and fit and so they act accordingly and like magic, they are.

It took me years to decode the truth. My big "aha!" was more of a process than a revelation but when I realized that I created these erroneous beliefs about food and self-image, I found the power to change them and in doing so, change my relationship with food and weight. I became the healthy, fit woman I was destined to be!

A belief, by definition, requires a leap of faith. Not always a big leap but a leap nonetheless. In a belief, there is an element of logic, which of course makes it feel very true. For instance, if you make plans for tomorrow, it is because you believe you are going to wake up tomorrow. This belief is based on the fact that you woke up this morning and the morning before, however, this doesn't make it true, it just makes it likely. There is a little leap of faith required that it will actually happen again.

So if everyone in your family is overweight, and you eat with them, share the same movement habits as them, and hold the same belief system as them, it is most LIKELY that you will be overweight as well. It doesn't make it true, just likely.

As we grew up, we took on beliefs about ourselves and our bodies based on evidence provided by someone we trusted or by our own personal experience. Today, if these particular beliefs no longer provide the outcome we desire, it's time to consider an upgrade.

Creating a new belief produces a new outcome. When I chose a new set of beliefs about my body, I got a new body. I took the leap of faith about a new genetic destiny where I had the creative power to change my body and become fit. Then my subconscious worked overtime to make me right about my new beliefs. What an amazing discovery this was!

These are the six steps I use to transform my beliefs, and ultimately, my body and health.

Take an inventory of your current beliefs.

Make a list of what you believe about your current physical fitness. How do you know what a belief is? A belief is a statement that sounds very true and often starts with "I am . . . " or "I can't . . ." Examples are things like "I'm fat," or "I can't exercise because I have a bad knee," etc.

Discover as many of these beliefs as you can. In fact, there are some key beliefs hiding behind big obvious ones that you can unlock if you go a little deeper.

Look at your list and highlight the standouts.

What beliefs do you recognize as being the most limiting? Yes, they are probably the ones that seem the most true but play along anyway. What have you got to lose? Now identify one current belief that no longer serves you.

Focus on what you want your new outcome to be.
If you want a body that is stronger, leaner or healthier, spend a few moments to write a description. What does it look like? What does it feel like? What do you do with it? How does that feel? Experience the details!

Design a new belief.
What would you have to believe about yourself and about your body to look and feel the way you want to? Use the power of your imagination to contemplate this. Pretend you already have that body and then imagine what your beliefs would be. Write the new beliefs down. Make sure they are all written in the positive. For instance, *I am strong*, versus *I am not weak*.

Live as if the new belief is true.
This step can be challenging but you can do it! Express your inner actor and act "as if." How would a person with your ideal body move in this world? What would they eat? How much sleep would they get? How would they treat themselves? How would they treat others? How often would they exercise? What kinds of thoughts would they have about exercise? What would their priorities be? What kinds of habits would they have?

Once you take action as if it is true, you adopt the habits and practices of the person with those positive beliefs and begin a sequence so magical, so inspired, that it leads to inevitable transformation!

SPOILER ALERT! Some of us want to believe that a person with this ideal body would eat perfectly, sleep perfectly, exercise perfectly . . . This is a lie designed to keep us from taking any action at all. Stop it!

Shift Your Beliefs to Get What You Want

Collect evidence that it is true.

As you live from this new belief system, keep a keen eye on all the evidence that proves you are right. Because you are.

What do you want to be right about? Choose that belief. It's no coincidence that BE is in the words BElief and BElieve. I like to think of them more as BE-LIFE and BE-LIVE. Gandhi said: "Be the change you wish to see in the world." Let's bring that home in this context with: "Be the life you want to live in the world."

My mom doesn't really worry about her weight anymore. We laugh about it together now as priorities change. She worries more about her heart and losing her marbles than fitting into a smaller pair of pants.

Me? I have chosen a life where I get to work in health and fitness with people who are transforming their bodies and their lives. I am grateful to be a part of it every day, as it is this work that helps me collect evidence that I am on my path. Once in awhile, I catch a glimpse of myself in a mirror and hear the echo of an outdated belief . . . and so I stop and look in the eyes of a scrawny twelve year old and I let her remind me . . . I am lovely.

About the Author

Melodee Meyer is a Mind/Body Fitness Trainer and Inspirational Speaker that coaches businesses, organizations and individuals on how to reclaim their bodies and their health through smart nutrition, exercise and positive mindset. She has her Masters Degree in Spiritual Psychology, is a Certified Nutritional Consultant and is a 5th Degree Black Belt recently inducted into the Karate Union Hall of Fame.

Melodee developed the award winning fitness program, Kickboxers Ultimate Training for people who want fast, extraordinary results. www.getKUT.com

She teaches her unique business systems and certifies instructors at trainings across the country.

Also known as Master Mel, she has a serious passion for people, animals and food — not always in that order. She blogs, teaches, writes articles and plays at Martial Arts Family Fitness, a center she owns with her family in Santa Barbara, CA.

www.MelodeeMeyer.com

Shift Your Beliefs to Get What You Want

Miracles Happen When You Love Yourself

Annie Lim

Seeing cockroaches running around on the food table in our dining hall during our recent trip to Cuba brought back memories of the place I lived and grew up in - my grandfather's shophouse that was built in the 1930s. What is a shophouse? Shophouses are commonly seen in South East Asia, they are mostly two stories high, where the ground floor is a shop and the second floor is used as the owner's residence. Back in the 70's, our kitchen was often visited by cockroaches at least 1.5" in length. I remember especially during nights when I was thirsty, I dreaded having to go downstairs to the kitchen to get some water.

Our "home" was pretty crowded. My grandfather, four uncles, my parents and my brother shared the four bedrooms on the second floor. Each room could only fit two twin beds so I slept outside in the hallway with my aunt on the floor. My mom and my aunt were both responsible for running the family business. The smell of coffee would seep up through the wooden floor to the second floor every morning at 5 am. My mom would always start by cleaning all the tables, chairs, utensils and kitchenware to ensure they were clean for the days' customers. She would prepare what was needed for the business and on top of that, prepare breakfast for my dad and us. After a long day of work at the coffee shop, my mom would then clean the house, make dinner and do the laundry for everyone. She typically went to bed at around 1am.

Being the eldest daughter in her family, she had to give up her education at the age of seven. She was expected to stay home to do all the housework and help out with the business.

Often, whenever she had some extra time, during moments when the coffee shop was not busy; she would promote different kinds of products to earn extra income for the family to make ends meet. Growing up seeing her work hard and always putting others first, somehow led me to create this belief that it was selfish to put yourself first and that it was very important to work very hard in order to be able to provide for the family.

Besides that, having grown up in a country where citizens of Chinese ethnicity are considered "visitors" made me feel like I didn't belong much of the time. This perception of "my people" had a profound impact on how I viewed others and myself. It was essentially this belief that motivated me to strive and work very hard in order to prove that I am worthy and deserving like everyone else; that I was good enough and that I had the right to be treated the same, equal and fair not because of my gender or ethnicity.

At an early age, I worked my butt off in school to earn good grades and I constantly strived to be the top performer. I went on to earn my degree with a magna cum laude, followed by recognition of being the top MBA student in the field of MIS. Feeling somewhat incomplete, I went on to tackle my PhD. I had my thesis published in internationally recognized business journals and am still very proud of that.

For a long time, I continue to collect certificate after certificate, thinking that it is what I need to show that I am capable. It was not until I reached a point in my life where I had a big wakeup call.

My Wake Up Call

I wanted to show the world that I was deserving and just as good. I worked hard, I worked long hours, I put my kids first, I put my family first, I wanted to make my parents proud of me and it got me nowhere! Clearly, my formula of working hard per se wasn't working, my degrees and certificates did not "fix" me. I asked myself, "What is missing?"

You see, fundamentally, I believed that I had to work hard, put others first before me and struggle in life, just like my mom did. I also believed that I was not good enough or deserving enough to have the life that I wanted. As a result, I unconsciously created a pattern in my life, to always work hard and not get what I wanted. Here is a classic example: The very first company I owned with my husband back in the year 2000 made $500k in a short three months. Well guess what happened. You've got it! We lost it all and beyond, and we had to struggle from then on, continuing this pattern for several years. In addition, with having two young children and constantly putting them first before my own needs, I got to a place of being overwhelmed and exhausted, I was crying often and not knowing why. I was sad most of the time.

Conversations That Make a Difference

It was when I had the A-Ha moment while I was working with my coach; I did not love myself, I was not grateful toward me, and I had neglected me. I then began a project of me appreciating me, a project I called "365 Days of Loving Myself."

You may have heard the saying, "In order to love others you have to love yourself first." When I first took on this project, I thought it was pretty ridiculous having to tell myself that I love myself. However, it was through this project where I realized that I had been really hard on myself — constantly pushing myself, not giving myself time for a break or time to take care of myself, and putting myself last on the list of all the people that needed to be loved and cared for. I discovered that I was insanely mean to myself! I was the biggest bully — not to others, but me. Not only was I not giving to or caring for myself, oh! The things that I said to myself were just cruel. I would tell myself how incompetent I am, how I don't know enough and am not ready to be able to move forward, how stupid I am for making mistakes, how I am not a good mother whenever I am not spending time with my children, the list went on and on and on like the Energizer bunny.

When I started the project, I began allowing myself to take time off. It started with short time span like ten minutes where I took time to read books, to just sit in the garden and breathe in fresh air. And as I grew comfortable with ten minutes, I began to stretch it out to twenty minutes and then thirty minutes and so on. I began to go for massages, started singing lessons, took time out with friends and I reassured myself that it was okay for me to take small vacations without my children.

I Put Myself First

I allowed myself to have fun and play, to have my inner child be nourished. I became more forgiving of my mistakes and accepting of who I was and who I wasn't. I became more grateful for what I had in life rather than forcing things to happen.

I had more compassion for myself and was less judgmental about things. As Dalai Lama said, "Love is the absence of judgment."

I learned to see that what I lacked was just a gap, and that there was nothing wrong with me, nothing to fix. I am perfect as is.

I learned to set boundaries and learned to say no so that I can have time for me, and not be obligated to take care of everyone else except myself.

I learned to ask for support and that it is okay to ask for support from friends and family. I learned that I don't have to do it alone and to figure out everything in life.

I learned to be vulnerable and open and authentic about my life with others.

Living this way has allowed me to be liberated. I felt freedom, peace and joy. Today, I can openly share with you that I enjoy calm, peace and joyfulness 90% of the time.

Loving myself and being free changed my relationships with my children, my husband, my business partners, money and so on...

I started creating the life I have always desired.

I started creating business partnerships that worked.

I created amazing vacations with my children. My favorite was the one I took my children out of school for four months (yes, you can absolutely do that!) and traveled all over South East Asia.

Conversations That Make a Difference

My relationship with my husband (I call him partner now!) shifted. I used to think that I needed him to be around for me. Now, I know I am whole and complete and we are together as partners in life because we enjoy each other's company and love each other, we are not there to please or complete each other.

I stepped into my own power and started to own my life. I am now madly in love with myself and I love my life more than ever. If what I have shared speaks to your heart, I want you to join me!

I invite you to do this exercise every day in the morning and evening. Take your hand and put in on your heart and feel love, and say to yourself "I love you." when you see yourself in the mirror. Tell yourself, "I am grateful for you."

I invite you to be madly in love with yourself. We are good at being in love with others, be it a celebrity, our love ones or children, and yet we forget to love ourselves. Perhaps, after reading my story you will consider taking on the "365 Days of Loving Myself" project for YOU! Do write to me at annie@drannielim.com and tell me more about your "love stories" and your practices.

Before I end this chapter, I just want to let you know that "I see you" for who you are, as in the movie, Avatar — "I see you." You have the power within to create the life you desire and deserve. You are powerful and amazing, with so much to love and be loved.

"Miracles happen when you love yourself!"

About the Author

Dr. Annie Lim is a serial entrepreneur, owning several businesses in various industries. Annie lives to serve and add value to the lives of others through her training, mentoring, coaching and consulting company www.DrAnnieLim.com. Annie started the WEWorld Summit, www.WEWorldSummit.com, a global online live summit and collaborative platform with the intention to create World Peace through Business by supporting women entrepreneurs and igniting HeartSoul entrepreneurship.

Annie has a PhD in Entrepreneurship with her research published in several notable international academic journals. She is a Cheri Blair Foundation business mentor and serves on the Board of Advisory for California Women's Conference.

Annie founded L.I.F.E. Children Foundation www.LIFEChildrenFoundation.org; an organization aiming to provide better educational opportunities to underprivileged children.

She adores her three children, Josiah, Jordan and Joy. She is the author of two forthcoming books on self-love and keys to powerful living. She enjoys singing, painting, travelling, reading and watching movies.

Born To Be Alive
Your Life, Your Message

Jim T. Chong

"Without purpose, we will never know if we've fulfilled our life's intent."

My hope is that in reading this, you will be able to live your life more intentionally...to LIVE STRONGER, BE MORE ENRICHED and DO MORE with your life because of the gratitude and appreciation gained through the foundation laid from the past generations and the clarity gained in looking towards the future. I would first like to share some stories of people whose life experiences have truly impacted me.

"Your personal alignment with your sense of purpose is arguably one of the most powerful forces that will propel you to do incredible things."

Defining our purpose positions us to do miraculous things; it helps define the "message of your life" to others. Discovering what you are passionate about is key to being able to really live and thrive in an intentional and fulfilling life. In my personal assessment, people that find their purpose tend to appreciate and want to do incredible things for others. A case in point is a wonderful friend named Mary Nicholson who was taken to a hospital due to a brain aneurysm followed by a stroke. The paramedics did not recognize the signs of the aneurysm and left her in the emergency waiting room unattended thinking she just had a bad headache even though her head was not able to support itself while she sat in the chair. It wasn't until one of Mary's friends finally arrived that she was given some attention when her friend called for help, as Mary was not able to communicate clearly.

Mary could have been paralyzed but by the grace of God, was able to relearn to walk and talk again with the help and love of her caregivers and friends. What does she do? Mary gets stronger from what life throws her way and finds her sense of purpose in saving other people's lives. She decided to create awareness about stroke and also a support system and resource for caregivers. Fast forward to several years later, with many obstacles to overcome, the awareness has now lead to several stroke centers recently being established in San Joaquin County's major hospitals as well as the formation of Healings In Motion, a non-profit dedicated to being a resource for stroke awareness/prevention and brain health. By sheer determination and a strong sense of what she was called to do, Healings In Motion has literally educated thousands of people about the signs of stroke and has also provided much needed resources to caregivers. Like Mary, those that can truly identify their purpose in life can really harness their life experiences to do incredible things.

Conversations That Make a Difference

Working with so many people from various ethnic backgrounds, I have seen people do what they do for a variety of reasons. Almost always though, those that are aligned with a cause are usually a magnet and catalyst for others to join the cause. They are usually more confident, more focused on what they are trying to accomplish, and raise up to be leaders by the life they live. What is the point? We should find the things that really resonate with us if we are to find our sense of purpose and fulfillment in life. Again, this helps you understand and deliver the "message of your life." What's the message you want to give?

"Cherish every moment in life. The memories and experiences can help you stay grounded and maybe even put a smile on your face."

As time goes by, I find myself transforming to be one that is learning to appreciate even more the things that I once ignored. For instance, it is easy to overlook the sacrifices made by those that truly care for us like our parents and close friends. Take time to consider the things you have to be thankful for. When you are able to tap into gratitude, you will find yourself happier, healthier, and more energized about life. At almost fifty years old at the time of this writing, I've learned so many things that I wish I would have known when I was younger. I see people taking time to reflect on the things that matter most...especially as they get older. Money and material things seem less important than appreciating the simple things, having a great friend to talk to, or just knowing you did something that helped someone else in some way.

Shift Your Beliefs to Get What You Want

    I find that my biggest motivation comes from those who know what they want their life to mean. Mai Nguyen, a powerful woman, showed me what community involvement really meant through her life's message. Mai decided she wanted to serve and make a big impact in her cultural community and has been influential in helping establish "Little Saigon" in South Sacramento. Like a drop of water in a pond, her positive actions have had created a wonderful and significant rippling in her community. I remember seeing the desire in her soul to make a big difference and put that passion into action...which translated into a tangible result.

    Another outstanding example is my good friend Chris Lambert, someone that has dedicated his life to serving recovering Veterans. Mr. Lambert, a three-time wounded in combat Marine, is a sought after speaker that helps you appreciate the freedom that you have and the sacrifices made for our country by our Veterans. I remember listening to his message on Memorial Day about how while we are enjoying the wonderful sounds of BBQ grills firing up, for many combat Veterans it can be very traumatic as the "popping" and igniting of the grills can bring back memories of them being in combat, having their comrades arms or head shot off. This may be graphic, but really connected with me on how I can take so much for granted and understand that, "Our freedom is not free."

    Taking time to reflect on the conversations and stories from those like Mai, Chris, and Mary lead me to appreciate their examples while also making some really wonderful friends along the way. My talks with them helped me shift my thinking into what is truly important and the lasting impact I could make.

Conversations That Make a Difference

"What's in YOUR Heart?"

I have definitely had my share of life's regrets which has helped make me stronger. I find that, absolutely, I do want to make my life count. One of the best ways I've discovered that helps me reach a variety of people in the shortest amount of time is public and cause based speaking. Growing up with numerous opportunities to inspire, motivate and educate, I found speaking to groups and organizations to be a great vehicle to touch many lives through stories and information. Being invited to facilitate and speak at hundreds of venues, I realized that when I am in front of people, I can have incredible impact if I take the time to craft messages that prompt people to not just think about the things that are important, but really to move them towards some sort of action.

*"Reflection is sometimes necessary to
see yourself clearly."*

I was blessed early in life to have been given many opportunities that would help me appreciate the potential we have to be almost anything we choose. My parents came from another country and did not speak English. The language barrier had them working harder than I ever would. In high school, I had competed and "trophied" in numerous debate and speech contests. These victories in speaking groomed me for my future years and proved to be one of the best "gifts" that I have been able to use. I have my Mom and Dad to thank for giving me so much; even though they came to this country with so little. Many doors have been opened for me to meet some of the people who have inspired me to action.

"A walk down memory lane can ground us and help us remember and appreciate what we have today."

Many things have evolved with time. We have seen the transition from the record albums to the iPods as well as the coming and going of Blockbuster Video to the $1 rentals at Red Box. However, one common theme has not changed — the desire for people to find their sense of purpose and live it out. For instance, the personal story of Sylvester Stallone is a very inspiring example of someone that fought against all odds for his dreams. We know Stallone's great success began with his movie *Rocky*. Did you know that this great actor made incredible sacrifices to have his dream realized? With very little money and great passion to be the lead actor in his own movie, Stallone was determined to make it happen despite being turned down repeatedly by Hollywood. Potential movie makers did not see him as a lead actor because of the way he talked.

When things got so bad for Stallone and his family, he sold his dog for a mere $50. Declining offers up to $400,000 for the *Rocky* script, Stallone settled for $25,000 which allowed him to star in the lead role. He was then able to locate the person to buy back his dog for $15,000. That's commitment to your dream! *Rocky* became one of the most iconic movies about personal victory, overcoming odds and of course being a champion! No matter how insignificant Stallone may have seemed in his desolate beginning, the *Rocky* movies have inspired millions across the globe. We all have the ability to impact others because of our relentless pursuit of our passions and commitment to fulfill our life's calling.

"Build TOGETHER, not alone... Create 'Win-Win' situations rather than 'Win For One'."

We work better and are stronger when we are in a community that supports our vision and alignment rather than working alone. In my time of need, I appreciate my best friends who were and are there for me!

Yes, indeed, I have always found myself somewhat gregarious — growing up loving to be around people — but in the past not really understanding why. I have been fortunate enough to be around powerful individuals who have helped me form Solutions4Life (S4L), an entity dedicated to serving cause based professionals and organizations supporting them in Health Care, Wealth Care, & Self Care and serves to support caused-based professionals and entities. Through collaboration and alignment with the right organizations and professionals, I find that life is much more rewarding when we are confident and KNOW that we can live our lives intentionally; to touch others and "Play Big." Take time to appreciate those around you and let it guide you to create your own legacy.

"Define it, Design it, and Live it!"

It really is a personal choice with endless possibilities to "Be the Positive Difference" to those around you. How many lives will you choose to change through your life's message and conversations? You have been "Born to Be Alive!"

About the Author

Jim T. Chong is a dynamic, community-centric individual focused on creating Win-Win strategies. He has trained and educated hundreds of financial professionals and clients and enjoys being an evangelist for financial literacy. Through his community involvement, his leadership and speaking venues, his desire is to help people connect, collaborate and succeed. Jim works with several recognized ethnic chambers and foundations and also serves on the Executive Board of Healings In Motion, a non-profit founded by Mary Nicholson dedicated to stroke awareness/prevention and brain health. In facilitating venues and presenting at various events and seminars, he consistently connects effectively with his audience that spans various age groups, cultures and communities. Jim's passion is to continually assist others to be a difference by helping them define and resonate their personal life message and create a personal roadmap to their success.

Jim is an Executive Speaker, Founder of Solutions4Life (S4L), Advanced Financial Solutions and a LTC Navigator.
Facebook: Jim T. Chong
http://www.jtcpresents.com
Contact Jim: 209.534.8000

Imperfection to Perfection: How I MANifested My Perfect Loving Soul Mate

Paula Hopwood

All I ever wanted was to be loved. I wanted to be loved with a love so deep and powerful that it would transport me to another world. I wanted to be able to see the love for me in a man's eyes. I wanted to feel that love with every fiber of my being. I wanted to be loved for who I was and not what I could do with my body. I was more than a physical body. My heart cried out to be heard. My soul longed to be cherished.

The men I knew were not capable of the love I so craved. I thought that if I wanted that type of love it must exist somewhere, right? A person does not just come up with something that does not exist, do they? I knew there must be someone out there that could love with wild abandon. "Yeah, right, Paula! Dream on," I would say to myself.

All I knew was that men used women for what they wanted, plain and simple. I had been taught from a young age that men were not to be trusted.

Shift Your Beliefs to Get What You Want

The day I was born, my father put me on a pedestal. Soon after that, I would be knocked off that pedestal to land with a crash.

My father always wanted a girl. I was born the baby, the precious baby girl, with two older brothers. I could do no wrong in my father's eyes. My brothers became jealous of me. I felt alone, let down, betrayed, and I knew I could not trust my brothers. For years I would try to win their love. I would try to win the love I so wanted from them. I eventually gave up, realizing that the love I wanted from my brothers did not exist.

When I was five years old, a fifteen year old male babysitter cemented my knowing that males could not be trusted. He forced himself on me. He taught me that men wanted one thing and that they would take it. That was just the way it worked.

When I was a teenager, my boyfriend would prove once again that males could not be trusted. Twice he took me without my permission. He didn't seem to care that I was hurting and crying out for help.

In the world that I lived in, the males would take, manipulate, control, and betray. Everyone that I knew, knew that. Men could not be trusted.

I went from one abusive relationship to another. I blamed the male. It couldn't be me. If I could just find the "right" guy, ALL my problems would go away. One of my problems though was that I thought there were no good guys. I thought that all men were not to be trusted. This was a problem. How would I ever have the love I dreamed of if I believed that men were incapable of providing it?

I met a guy who convinced me he loved me. I felt something was off. He wasn't always nice and he called me names. He never put me first. He was very selfish. But he said he loved me. So I thought maybe marrying him was the answer.

I spent eleven years married to someone who did not love me. He thought he loved me. He possibly even wanted to love me. He didn't love me though, and it showed. Every time he would do or say something to hurt me, he would kill me a little inside. I felt that, if I had his child, he would love me. I gave birth to two beautiful boys in those 11 years. This made his abuse worse. I begged him to take couples' counseling with me. He shot me, and our relationship, down repeatedly. I tried everything I could think of to help the marriage be a loving one. He always took great pleasure in attacking me and my ideas. He was killing me slowing and surely. I became angry, depressed, and suicidal. Eventually I developed a "way out" of that loveless abusive marriage.

When I realized that my belief that "there are no good men" was attracting into my life more of what I didn't want, that was the day I realized I needed to shift my belief. So instead of focusing on what I did not want, I started to focus on what I truly wanted. I put my order out to the Universe of what I truly desired and what I truly deserved. I created my own dream man in my head.

When my real life husband would hurt me verbally, physically, sexually, emotionally, spiritually, and mentally, I would visualize being honored and loved by my dream man.

I always called my dream man my "perfect" man. I didn't know what he looked like and I only wanted what was best for me. He was perfect for me. So my perfect dream man did not have a face or a name.

I will tell you something though — my perfect man loved me with a passion unheard of. His perfect love filled every

Shift Your Beliefs to Get What You Want

hole in my soul that every male had ever made. I loved daydreaming about him and making a list of his special qualities. I did this all in my head. I did not want to get caught talking about my perfect man while I was married to my real-time husband.

I didn't tell anyone about my perfect man I dreamt of. I did not want them to laugh at my foolishness. I did not want anyone to ruin the feelings I had and taint my perfect dream. Nope...no one was going to take his perfect love away from me. I kept my list of his perfect qualities in my head. I added to that list whenever I was hurt, angry, frustrated — so pretty much all the time.

My perfect man loves me with a love that never fails.
My perfect man puts me first...in everything.
My perfect man does not give up.
My perfect man shines his love for me out of his eyes with such intensity.
When my perfect man holds me in his arms, I know I am safe, secure, cherished, and loved.
My perfect man has big wide shoulders with arms that wrap around me in fierce devotion and love.
My perfect man calls me by the sweetest love nicknames.
My perfect man is the right height to complement my size.
My perfect man smells so, so good.
When my perfect man talks, his voice is deep and powerful, just like him.
My perfect man sings in a deep voice, off key, and it is the sexiest thing I have ever heard.
My perfect man loves my children as his own.
My perfect man is spontaneous and adventurous.

Conversations That Make a Difference

When my perfect man makes love with me, it is so tender and full of his love for me that I feel it in every fiber of my being.
Peace and love live in my perfect man's heart.

I would visualize and fantasize about being in the presence of my perfect man. I could feel his love. I could feel how he made me feel. I could feel him…my perfect man.
Then I started to daydream about being in his presence and about some of the things we would do:

We went horseback riding together.
We went camping together.
We traveled the world together.
We tried new things together.
We watched movies and just cuddled together.
We just loved being together.

My perfect man loves me, our relationship, and our future.
"Too bad he is only in your head, Paula," I would tell myself.
But when I was hurting, I would go to my list and feel love. I would experience what I thought love should really be. I would feel the love I craved so badly. At least there, in my head, my heart could feel what it longed for. My soul could rest easy knowing it was loved and feeling that love.
Soon one thing led to another. The abuse was getting too hard for me to bear. I tried ending my pain many times. I just couldn't do it. I could not leave my boys. So I made a decision to live positively. I didn't know where that decision was going to take me.

Shift Your Beliefs to Get What You Want

From the first day of our marriage, my husband threatened me with divorce almost daily. That would make me cry and feel unloved. Somehow he liked that. After I made my decision to be positive, something changed within me. The next time he threatened me with divorce, I took him up on his offer.

I found myself a single mom with two little boys to care for. Every guy in the country was after me for some reason. I didn't trust them. I thought they didn't know me well enough and only wanted sex from me. So I decided to date a male friend — someone who I kind of trusted. I had two male friends at the time that seemed nice. Could I trust them? I told them that I was going to start dating and that if they were interested to let me know. I told them I only wanted to take it one day at a time and that I was not looking for marriage. I told them that my love tank was empty, and I was only looking for someone to hold my hand, hold me, and tell me I am beautiful.

They both took this well. One was looking for a wife and scared me with how excited he got about me being in that role. The other friend did not say a word. He just bought me a rose and held my hand quietly. There was such strength and passion in his eyes. I knew I wanted to be with him.

I started dating Patrick that night. I thought I was crazy. He was 7 years younger than I was. Seven years! I felt like I was garbage and used up, that no one would want me. That is what had been drilled into me by my first husband. Why would this young bright man want to date me?

Two months into dating him, I realized Patrick had everything on my list. Everything. I had known Patrick for a couple of years and had never realized this. Our relationship grew. We had obstacles to overcome. He never gave up and he wouldn't let me give up either. We grew together and had two more children. We have been married ten years now. We love each other with a passion that grows daily. When problems come our way, we only have solutions and love for each other.

I am loved, cherished, honored, accepted, and I feel his love for me in every fiber of my being. His love and support have helped me to heal and grow into the woman I was made to be.

I realized that I actually called our relationship into being. The words I said and the emotions I felt when I was escaping the other relationship are all real now. I did not know anything about manifesting or the law of attraction when I was doing this. I was just hurting so badly and needed a way out. I made my list as if this man existed. Little did I know he did exist. Or that he was someone I knew.

I made my list and I was careful with the words I used. I was creating my perfect soul mate. I did not use future words like "want" and "will." I had my fill of wanting. The words I chose were present tense words like "has," "is" and "does." When I thought of my perfect man, I felt the feelings I wanted in my real life. I felt them in my real dream world that I had created.

My mind, heart, and soul were being fed love and I was so thankful. I now know that a big reason I was able to manifest my perfect man was because I became the person who could live in such a relationship. I had made the decision to be positive. It had all started with me.

I knew what I wanted. I knew how it felt. I had even lived it in my mind. I was so thankful for the experience. And what I focused on became my reality.

Shift Your Beliefs to Get What You Want

With a shift in belief on my part, I went from repeating imperfect relationships to living a life with perfection and lots of love from my true soul mate — the man I MANifested.

About the Author

Paula Hopwood is an inspirational speaker, coach and author whose life is all about turning dreams into reality.

Coming from an abusive background Paula changed her whole mindset from one of extreme negativity to one of abundance, transformation, and love.

Change is inevitable; however growth is optional. When Paula discovered this she left her negative mindset behind and made the choice to become the person she had always envisioned she could be.

Along the way Paula learned the necessary lessons to set a person free from the bondage of negativity and now shares these most important lessons with people from all walks of life.

Paula helps people to realize their dreams and live life to the fullest.

As Paula says, "Life is for living — bring it on!!"

Paula now enjoys her life with her loving supportive husband and 4 amazing inspiring children.

Please contact Paula at www.paulahopwood.com

Shift Your Beliefs to Get What You Want

From Crazed to Clarity and Compassion

Rosie Aiello

I hate the word forgive. It's overused. If one more person tells me I have to forgive my ex-husband, I'm going to punch them. They have no idea what hell I went through. I can never forgive him. He tortured me, for heaven's sake. Forgiveness and this man cannot appear together. Never. I wish people would mind their own business and drop this forgiveness thing.

Five years earlier…

My husband and I are having a delightful lunch on our balcony overlooking the city of Beirut and the beautiful Mediterranean Sea. We are blessed to enjoy this glorious view daily. A cottony, brown layer hovers over the city tarnishing the skyline on occasion; but this day, the sky is a clear, baby blue. The sea sparkles in the sunlight. This summer day is blistering hot, even high on the mountain where we live. What is better than a nice, cold slice of sweet, juicy watermelon to quench that heat?

As I serve a slice of watermelon to my husband, he casts his eyes down annoyingly. Unenthused he picks up his fork and knife and begins to eat. Something seems off with him now. We had been having a lovely lunch together, and then all of a sudden with no warning he displays a sudden mood shift. I did not ask him if anything were wrong. I desperately try to hang onto the wonderful feeling I was experiencing only moments before. He does not look at me. We eat the remainder of our lunch in silence. When he finishes eating, he stands up, says a perfunctory thank you and leaves.

    I sit alone, bewildered and confused. My stomach instantly turns into a knot as I hold back the tears. The watermelon I was so eagerly looking forward to savoring rests untouched. I become despondent, as this is the millionth time he has behaved this way. Yet despite more than 20 years of living with this man, I still cannot figure out what prompts his dramatic mood shifts and anger. "What have I done wrong?" I would ask myself each and every single time these episodes would occur. I knew I was in trouble, yet I forced myself to shove the incident out of my mind and continued my best to enjoy the rest of the day.

    The following day in the afternoon, I thought I would offer a kind gesture to my husband by bringing up a piece of cold watermelon to his office. His home office faces west, which becomes like an oven by the late afternoon. I hand him the watermelon, and again I see this horrible scowl. Dreading conflict with him I nevertheless push myself to ask what is wrong. If I don't ask, I know "it" will brew into a spewing volcano. I choose the lesser of two evils. Clearly annoyed, he replies that the watermelon is "cut wrong." I think to myself, "Cut wrong? How do you cut a watermelon wrong?" He begins to explain to me how he wants the watermelon sliced. His "explanation" is not a simple sentence or two, it is a mini-tirade. "Okay," I say as complacently and agreeably as possible, yet thinking, "What else can he possibly conjure up to complain about?" I slither out of the room, like a beaten dog.

That evening after dinner, our housekeeper serves us watermelon. I had forgotten to tell her how to cut it. "Oh, shit," I think. "I'm going to get it." Angered, my husband yells at me and instructs me never to have her cut watermelon anymore. He screams that he will show us how to slice it properly. His rage renders me motionless as I sit and listen to his angry outburst — over how to cut a watermelon, for hrissakes! I cannot believe my ears. Who creates a tirade about how to cut a watermelon? Nevertheless I sit frozen in fear. I eke out a sincere sounding, "I am sorry. I will remember from now on how to properly cut the watermelon." Silently, I beg God to give me peace.

He never does take the time to gives us a "lesson" on how to cut it.

Confusion becomes my closest companion. My damn left analytical mind demands that I understand how things work, or don't work. My head throbs and spins, challenging one theory after another. His behavior makes no sense. He's charming, playful, funny and the life of the party. Yet, in a blink of an eye he becomes an emotional, sucking, raging vampire. He's very smart. He has a Ph.D. after all. He's an engineer. He's logical. Yes, he's right. I've got to do better, be better. Then things will be good.

I hunker in my bathroom, separate from his, and lock the door. It's the only place in the house where I can seek solace and peace. I sit on the toilet seat, my head in my hands, tears flowing down, silently. I don't want our daughter to hear me. "Why can't I learn to do things right? What's wrong with me?" I scream in my head. "Why can't I remember to do things the right way? Then he wouldn't be upset at me so often. I don't want to make him angry. I'm really trying — all the time." I tell myself repeatedly that I can get through this. I must save this marriage and hold this family together. I'm feeling like I am going C-R-A-Z-Y.

Exhaustion. Depression. Nausea. Hopelessness. Despair. Craziness. I hate these constant companions. I hate all of them.

The following day, my husband is happy as a lark. He's joking and being playful with me. I thought he was furious at me. My head is bursting trying to figure out mood reversal. He acts as if nothing over the two prior days ever occurred. As if he didn't have those angry outbursts over the watermelon. As if he forgot that he gave me the silent treatment for two days. Now, I need to be happy and take advantage of these moments when he is happy. The whole house is happy when he's happy.

And so my life went on for nearly twenty-five years of being with this man — an emotional roller coaster ride that twisted and tormented my mind. I didn't know right from wrong. I doubted my feelings and beliefs. I was miserable. I didn't know what I was doing wrong.

I began to live in a constant state of fear. I was scared to do anything that I thought might upset him. I tried to remember all his new daily rules. I was scared to breathe wrong in front of him. I started to avoid him so I wouldn't cross his path the wrong way and give him a reason to hurl his anger.

Yet, I wanted this marriage to work. We had a child together. You have to stay together for your child. That's what good parents do; they stay together for the sake of the children.

Until your child (in my case, an adult child six months shy of turning 21) tells you, "Mom, you have got to take me away from my abusive father."

Shift Your Beliefs to Get What You Want

My daughter's demand ignited action. I, therefore, planned and executed the escape of our lives — an escape that began in Beirut, Lebanon and ended in San Francisco, California. We had finally broken the chain of the daily mental torture that had nearly destroyed both my twenty-one year old daughter and me.

That was five years ago.

Acclimating to new surroundings, going through legal proceedings, discovering how I was going to survive financially and undergoing trauma therapy were challenging enough. It was too much to bear when I was told that I should forgive. I didn't understand when they told me I needed to forgive myself. My ears screamed when I heard I needed to forgive my ex-husband, the man who emotionally tormented and tortured me for a quarter century. I entered a conflicted state: How can I, in my heart, forgive a man who not only tormented me, but also my daughter, my precious innocent child? Forgiving seems to be the buzz word of the new millennium. That topic fills magazines. Oprah talks about it. I kept thinking, "They don't know my story. They don't know what I went through. How dare they tell me I need to forgive?"

I do not believe that time alone heals. I made concerted efforts to search different avenues to recover. In addition to my trauma therapist, I worked with a holistic healer. I became a voracious reader of books and listened to or watched various media about meditating and how to change my way of thinking, and I learned ways to empower myself. The Law of Attraction, Rhonda Byrne, Dr. Brian Weiss, Dr. Deepak Chopra, Dr. Wayne Dyer, Louise Hay and others became my new constant companions. The teachings were uplifting and empowering. I felt like a child in a candy store devouring this amazing and powerful knowledge. These shifts in perspective redirected my view on life.

Then that word forgiveness percolated up again.

I kept hearing: "You need to forgive yourself."

Really, what did I do?

They said, "Forgiving is not about the other person, it's about you."

What do you mean? It is about the other person. I have to forgive what he did to me. It is all about the other person.

"Forgiving the other person doesn't mean you accept that what he did was okay."

Now I'm really confused because forgiveness to me means you accept what the person did, and despite his actions you still forgive him. This is HARD.

All this forgiveness talk and new definitions or new explanations of old definitions were challenging my beliefs and thinking.

Then, nearly four years after working on me, the moment came when I could tolerate accepting the word forgiveness into my vocabulary.

I blamed myself for marrying this man in the first place. I blamed myself for staying with him in order to keep my daughter in a whole family. Then I forgave myself; it felt like a release of a spring.

I was far from forgiving my ex-husband though.

Arriving at clarity took time, guidance, work, and determination.

A mentor explained: When you do not forgive, you continuously expend energy to hold that person in the jail of your mind. When you release those ill feelings, you release that energy you were using to hold him in there. Forgiveness relieves you. Or, as others said, it's like you are getting ready to throw a hot coal at your oppressor, yet you are the one getting burned in the meantime. When I grasped the significance of forgiveness from this new perspective, I was open to forgive my ex-husband.

The moment came when it was not so much that I needed to forgive my ex-husband so that I could move forward, but that I now felt the urge to forgive him. I knew I was coming from a completely different place.

When I forgave him, I released that hold of resentment I was harboring against him, discharging that sucking energy of making him a prisoner in my mind. I am freed. What an exuberant feeling!

Not only do I forgive and harbor no ill feelings towards my ex-husband, I hold compassion for and thank him for teaching me many important life lessons: for teaching me how to speak my truth, for teaching me how to set and maintain my boundaries, for making me realize my life purpose, and for making me realize and experience for the first time in my life how truly wonderful life is and all that it has to offer. What wonderful gifts I have received!

What I know for sure: Forgiveness released the prison I was holding myself and my ex-husband in. Now, my life is expanding and becoming more fulfilled with each passing moment. My heart glows with love, appreciation and gratitude.

I guess that forgiveness stuff is not so bad after all.

About the Author

Rosie Aiello
MBA, productivity expert, small business mentor, speaker and author is the founder of ClearVista Consulting International, Inc. With more than 30 years of experience, her clients improve their time management skills, are more productive, have higher profits and less stress following the systems that Rosie has developed.

Rosie@ClearVistaConsulting.com
www.ClearVistaConsulting.com
Phone: 415.939.7876

From Loss to Love

MarBeth Dunn

"The deeper that sorrow carves into your being, the more joy you can contain. Is not the cup that holds your wine the very cup that was burned in the potter's oven? And is not the lute that soothes your spirit, the very wood that was hollowed with knives?"
~ *Khalil Gibran, The Prophet*

Valentine's Day, 2009 was the day my life changed forever. I was happy. I had a small practice as an energy healer, empathy, and intuitive and I taught an occasional workshop. My relationship with my sweetheart was easy and uncomplicated. Life was good.

I awoke that fateful morning feeling strangely agitated, in a heightened state of awareness. Curiously, I found myself sending life force energy to Harold though I was barely awake. Harold's mom had passed away ten days earlier, and I assumed I had connected with him empathically to bless him with the healing love he needed. He was a fun, quirky sports aficionado in a baseball cap, who had lived his passion as a lighting director for such notables as Kris Kristofferson,

Conversations That Make a Difference

Jakob Dylan and the Wallflowers, and the Brian Setzer Orchestra. He was fond of saying, "I have a great career behind me."

I had left Harold the night before, returning home for an early morning figure drawing class. On the way to class, I was astounded to hear myself pleading passionately, tearfully, "Take this relationship!" I cried, "And make of it what You want it to be. I'm releasing it into Your Hands. I love him, but I'm releasing him to You." I could not grasp why the words came out of my mouth, or why I was so emotional.

At the studio, while setting up my easel, I stopped for a moment to chat with a friend. Suddenly lightheaded, I felt unsteady, disoriented, suspended in time, as I held on to a table to keep from falling to the floor. The feeling lasted momentarily and then I was normal again, just slightly shaken and uneasy.

Looking back, I understand that I had helped Harold transition. First, I let him go. Then, at the moment he left his body, I left mine, to be with him. I was able to split my consciousness, so that I could be with Harold, and in the drawing group simultaneously. And although I did not know this was even possible, Michael Newton, Ph.D. describes it brilliantly in *Journey of Souls: Case Studies of Life Between Lives.*

"A curious phenomenon about the spirit world is that important people in our lives are always able to greet us, even though they may already be living another life in a new body."

In his book, Newton presents the firsthand accounts of twenty-nine people placed in a "super-conscious" state of awareness through deep hypnosis, where he was able to access their hidden memories of life in the spirit world after physical death.

I had met death up close and personal before this, losing both my grandparents and my mom, but this was very different. It was shocking, unexpected and devastating. Harold and I had plans for a romantic concert that evening, and when I was unable to reach him during the day, I drove to his home, only to find him lying face down on the floor. His death wrenched my heart open and, like Pandora, I had no way to shove the profusion of painful emotions and experiences back into the box.

Now, as I look back, my most important realization is that no matter what life hands me, I always have a choice as to how I respond.

On many levels, it would have been so easy to succumb to this tragedy, and curl up in a ball of grief. Yet I knew in the depths of my soul, that I might not emerge for a long, long time if I did. My heart told me to move forward, and I knew Harold did not want me to grieve for long. His lighthearted spirit made that abundantly clear after his passing.

You see, there was the seminar I'd been planning to attend for months, scheduled a week after Valentine's Day. No one would have faulted me for canceling, yet I knew I had to go. Reeling from grief and ill with bronchitis, I desperately needed the "girl time" and support from my three, very dear and powerful friends who stayed with me for the event. And, although it was not easy to wrest my mind away from my tragedy to focus on the seminar, the presentation was lively and interactive which helped immensely.

I was not at my best, in fact I felt singularly unattractive, so I was quite astonished to be approached by the most attractive man in the room, who wanted to work with me during a practice session. Puzzled, I agreed. I became increasingly bewildered as several men lined up behind him to practice with me. As I finally returned to my seat, the man seated in front swiveled around to chat. That did it. I stood and walked to the rest room while a voice inside my head sang *I'll take care of you,* an obscure song Harold had given me. Despite my grief, I could not help chuckling. "Thanks for sending me all the men," I said. "Harold, it is way too soon for me! I do appreciate the thought, though."

Moving forward was not easy. There were days when I was crushed beneath an avalanche of emotions. There were days when I was overcome with guilt. Why did I not make him go to a doctor when I knew something was wrong? I should have done something. Anything! Somehow this had to have been my fault. Nevertheless, I was able to release the guilt. I was blessed with the training and ability to use a wide range of techniques for releasing painful emotions easily and effectively. Surprisingly, it was not long before I had moved through my process. My heart was healed. The love was still there and I had beautiful memories of a sweet and gentle man. I felt good!

And that's when it hit me. Millions of people despair in grief, sadness, pain and fear and don't realize they have a choice. Yet I had just blazed a path through my emotional catastrophe gracefully, and in a relatively short time. In my hands I held a precious key to release their pain. What if I could guide them through pain and grief into joy and happiness?

Eureka! I had discovered my Purpose at last!

An ancient yogic Sutra from the great Patanjali tells us that everything in life, whether it appears to be a positive or negative experience, is essentially a gift. We can choose how to perceive it. Having come through my trial by fire, I can now see the many benefits inherent in my experience of Harold's passing, though at the time, I would have probably smacked anyone for suggesting that there could possibly be anything positive in all the pain.

Discovering my purpose was only one of the many blessings I received from this experience that changed me forever.

I have grown and expanded in so many ways.

I have a deeper sense of myself.

I have a deeper connection with our Creator

I find that I am more compassionate and have a greater understanding of myself and others.

I have a greater capacity for joy.

I have a greater reverence for life.

I am gentler with myself

I know at a deeper level that love conquers death and that love is forever.

I am more confident in myself and my ability to handle life's vicissitudes

I feel more connected with all of humanity.

I am aware, appreciative and grateful for the many beautiful friends and family, who reached out to love and support me during my process.

It's never easy to lose someone you love. Yet it is important to know that in every instant you have the power to decide whether to lament and suffer or to choose the path to happiness.

I've noticed that many people feel the need to grieve for a specific amount of time to honor their loved ones, and that's okay. Yet I truly believe your loved ones don't want you to suffer. Were the situation reversed, with you leaving your beloveds behind, would you want them to be well and happy, and to move on with life? Or would you want them buried in a blanket of suffering and grief? It's always your decision, of course. Whatever you decide, treat yourself gently.

It can be incredibly freeing to honor your loved one by creating a legacy, a memorial to perpetuate their memory. Some people create a fund or raise money to support a cause dear to their loved one. Others might create a garden, or a painting. I compiled a photo album of Harold's life and our time together. Every person who hears my message and shakes off the shackles of pain, grief, sadness, anger or guilt is a testament to his beautiful spirit.

The greatest gift that Harold gave me was letting me know that it was okay to move forward. In fact, he encouraged it. His love will always shine within me, making me a better, richer person for having known him. I will continue to honor his memory by helping others break free and recognize their magnificence.

About the Author

MarBeth Dunn is known as the Joy to Abundance Strategist and the TV Happiness Coach. Her gift of empathy and intuition pinpoint the issues keeping you stuck, and assist you in accessing greater confidence, alignment, financial freedom, and closer, more harmonious relationships with yourself and others. Working with her, you will learn to engage your empathic and extra-sensory abilities, to create new realities, fulfilled desires, and unlimited possibilities.

Host of Having it All with MarBeth Radio, MarBeth's inspiring work has been featured on several television networks, including FOX, NBC, CBS, and WEYW 19, Key West, where she is a frequent guest.

MarBeth has recently established the Institute for Empathic Development.

Download her free eBook, *7 Steps to Get Unstuck and Unlock Your Joy* at www.yourjoyjourney.com.

Learn more about MarBeth at www.marbethdunn.com.

Let's Talk About
From Death Do Us Part to Life That We Live

Shawneen Rubay

Twenty-five percent of us will die unexpectedly. Seventy-five percent of us will die from disease or natural causes. Either way, none of us are getting out alive. So, if that's how things really are, then why do we have so much trouble talking about it?

What if talking about death could actually inspire us to live — to really live? What if facing the unthinkable or looking straight into the eyes of the dragon opened up a whole new world of possibilities and inspired us to dream bigger? What if making our final plans and getting our affairs in order could actually help us with our present plans?

There is nothing like hearing the words, "You have cancer," to remind you that this body and this life on earth are finite. That is what happened to me in 2004. There was nothing that could have prepared me for that moment. I don't think that there ever is. My first thought was, "What if I die from this?" Will I live to see my three children grow up? Our youngest son, Alec, was in the third grade at the time and his high school graduation seemed like a lifetime away.

In the back of my mind, I was also thinking about the friends and relatives that I knew that had battled cancer their whole lives. Was that going to be my future? I was fortunate that at the age of 37, my stage 1B breast cancer was treatable with a good prognosis. However, facing treatment, and looking at other cancer patients with a different prognosis really opened my eyes to my own mortality. It was facing my own mortality that catapulted me right smack dab in the middle of the present moment. When you are being presented with life or death options there is little or no time to put anything off. The experiences on which you are about to embark upon become more like baptism by fire. Courage is not an option. You must become fearless.

One night, following one of my chemotherapy treatments, I picked up a book that my surgeon had given to me. It was a book that was written by a team of experts, including my doctor. One of the final chapters dealt with the process of "letting go." I had noticed the chapter in the table of contents and while reading the other chapters, I kept it in the back of my mind. I knew that I would encounter it soon enough. It was aimed toward women with late stage diagnoses and I knew that it was going to be difficult to read. Like many of us, I avoided the thought of dying as much as possible. It seemed neither helpful under the circumstances nor a subject that was in alignment with a person who needed to maintain a positive outlook. In spite of this, I decided that ignorance was not bliss in this situation and I owed it to myself and to my family to become informed. That night, I made the decision to read it. I could feel the anxiety in my entire body. I had the irrational thought that if I read it and acknowledged it, then somehow it could become my reality. Irrational? Sure, but letting go, to me at the time, sounded a lot like giving up.

Conversations That Make a Difference

What I discovered next would change everything. I discovered that by NOT focusing on the outcome, I could experience the joys of today. It seemed like a simple enough concept, and yet it was such a challenge to detach from the outcome and just experience the moment taking place RIGHT NOW. By facing the idea of letting go of things that I could not control gave me a new sense of freedom. This was something that I had never known before.

By being more present, I started to notice the multiple layers of daily life experiences. My life had been one of details and obligations but now I was waking up to every day miracles. Simple tasks that I had done for years became gifts that I no longer took for granted. Being a few minutes late to piano lessons really didn't seem to matter to me anymore. Taking the extra time to listen to my children's stories of their school day became much more important. I started to savor these moments and to live life more fully with a new sense of wonder and gratitude. I began to rediscover passions that I had tucked away, hoping that I would return to them sometime in the future. I enrolled in culinary school, I started sewing again and I began volunteering at non-profit organizations. I felt ALIVE!

Facing my own mortality and seeing every aspect of life as meaningful DREW ME to "end of life work." I became a hospice volunteer by training with the Twilight Brigade and later trained to become a Death Midwife.

My goal is to impart to you what I have learned and give you some tools to help you face death with a new perspective that will allow you to more fully live in the present moment.

The first step in being able to discuss death is to become comfortable with the realization that we are all going to die. Our social culture keeps it at a distance so that it gets entirely removed from the present and is sent off into some future dimension. Why not take it out of the shadows and break the silence to allow it to teach us more than what we thought that we knew?

Life Review

As a hospice volunteer, one of my roles is to bear witness to people facing their last rite of passage by being an effective listener. In the present moment, one of the best gifts that you can give someone is to listen to him or her. Our hope is that by allowing the patient to discuss their life experiences, they will come to see their life as beautiful and complete. We refer to this as life review. The goal of life review with hospice patients is to reaffirm their self worth. The technique involves helping clients review their lives to affirm their existence and to bring closure. It seeks to resolve old conflicts that prevent them from moving forward without regret and it encourages them to attend to any unfinished business. We focus on their positive accomplishments and help them to see their contributions to the world. This enables them to see the legacy that they are leaving behind. The feeling that they have given something that has made a difference to the world and to their friends and loved ones brings validation. It is a powerful tool in helping them to come to terms with who they have been and to bring joy and fulfillment to the time that they have left. This can be conducted in an interview process, (Life Interview) or over the course of several visits. It can be made into an audio recording or even a video recording.

For a hospice patient, this life review comes at the end of his/her life, but we can all take advantage of this useful tool by conducting periodic life reviews at any stage of our lives.

In looking back, we can identify powerful milestones and meaningful events. We can reassess and reshape our thinking about life, and make any adjustments to our present course. It allows us to determine if we have any unresolved conflicts, giving us an opportunity to move forward to improve relationships and to repair misunderstandings. It reminds us of those items on our "bucket list" that are yet to be accomplished and dreams that are still waiting to materialize.

It allows us to embrace and appreciate the meaning of our life story. And along the way, we may discover some life-changing insights to help direct us through our own futures.

Writing your Eulogy

A eulogy is a written speech praising the accomplishment of someone who has recently died. Eulogies may be given as part of funeral services. They usually take place in a funeral home during or after a wake. It is offered as a tribute to the family and friends of the deceased and is a cherished tradition that has been around since the 16th century.

Similar to a life review, writing your own eulogy allows you to summarize pivotal and transformational periods in your life. By writing it down, we can ask ourselves, "Is this how I would like my story to end?" This can provide key information in plotting our future courses and allow us to see our life's purpose in a more concise way.

Expressing Gratitude

When working with hospice patients, there is really no time like the present to express love and appreciation to friends and family members who have touched our lives. This usually involves writing letters or making telephone calls to articulate the impact that an individual has made on our lives. These expressions of gratitude can be directed toward family members, friends, teachers, employers and anyone along the way that enriched their lives. By acknowledging the support and love that was shown to them over time, they begin to feel a profound sense of value and contentment. We can all benefit from cultivating more gratitude in our lives. Why not let someone know today that they have made an impression on your life and that some of who you are is because of them?

Letting Go

I shared with you the importance of letting go so that I could start to see my own experiences in a more meaningful way. Letting go is a term that we use in end of life work. Family members will express to their loved ones that it is okay for them to let go. In some cases, it's even encouraged to give your loved one permission to go. It can be a difficult task from every perspective, but it is this act of surrender that allows us to be fully present in the moment. It allows us to release past judgments about others and ourselves so that we can immerse ourselves into the beauty of what is taking place right in front of us.

Closing Thoughts

Having cancer changed me and I will never be the same. When I reminisce about that time, I truly believe that it was a gift that gave me more joy and renewed sense of purpose. You don't need to have a terminal illness or close encounter with death to start you thinking about the things that really matter most to you. You can begin now. You can experience the gifts of the present moment right now. If you are facing a serious illness or if you are receiving end of life support right now, just remember that time is only a number and none of us really know when our time is up. The present moment is all any of us really have. Let's be inspired! Let's choose to live NOW!

Shift Your Beliefs to Get What You Want

About the Author

Shawneen Rubay is the co-founder and Executive Director of Justin Time Children's House, a non-profit that provides art expression and support groups to children and their families who have that have experienced the death of a loved one.

She has worked with several non-profits in Los Angeles County with expertise in events and fundraising.

Shawneen is a wife and mother of three wonderful children.

She is a ten-year breast cancer victor. Having faced her own mortality, Shawneen found herself drawn to end of life issues. Inspired by her personal experience she chose to become certified by the Twilight Brigade and serves at the bedside as a hospice volunteer and a Death Midwife.

Contact Shawneen Rubay:
www.justintimechildrenshouse.org
info@justintimechildrenshouse.org
Facebook: Justin Time Children's House
Twitter: Shawneen Rubay
Phone: 661-297-0340 (USA)

Shift Happens
Believing is Seeing

Candi Parker

What would you do if you knew that you could have anything you want? It has been said, "All things are possible to those that believe." Do you believe that? This is not easy for some people. They are so focused on what they don't have in their lives that it can be difficult to believe that they can have the life they really want. Many people continually have their focus on what went wrong in the past and the jealousy, guilt, shame, blame emotional drama that they hold on to like a security blanket day in and day out.

And then there is the disbelief that what you believe creates your reality. I think some people are afraid to believe they can actually have what they want so they won't be greatly disappointed. So, what is the opposite of fear? It's Faith!

If you believe in miracles, then you experience miracles. If you believe something will not work, it won't. Teach yourself to believe in possibilities and to believe that what you really want is possible and is already on its way to you. Why not try it? It does take practice. If I told you that you could play the guitar like a pro, you wouldn't expect it to happen on the first try would you? No, of course not. First, you would have to get used to something new. You would learn and practice a lot and then, depending on how much you have made it a part of your everyday life, you could be a pro. The same is true with anything you want to learn.

Yes, you can learn to shift your beliefs to something that will serve you better. It just means you have to root out the beliefs you currently hold and decide if they are still working for you. Then CHOOSE new thoughts. With practice you manifest what you want.

As with anything, you really do get better at it with practice. Accept where you are now and believe that you are growing into a new you. Rather than worry about HOW something happens, focus on WHAT you want to see happen.

Our beliefs are quite embedded in us. They are created from the time we are born and we also carry the memories and traditions of our ancestors. We are imprinted from our parents, grandparents, teachers and peers by *their* beliefs. From the time I was a little girl I was taught to be a wife and mother through children's stories and toys as well as what I was taught at home, and that a man will take care of me and we will live happily ever after. You know the fairy tale. Because of these beliefs imprinted upon us, girls have expectations that are not usually met.

At age fifty-three I had a chance for a do over. It was shortly after my brother was murdered and my husband died that I had to learn a new way of living. I decided to consciously direct my life. I wanted to be able to take care of myself. I had come to realize just how short life can be and I wanted my time here to be quality time. I had my mind, my attitude and my imagination. I could choose how I looked at my life and imagine the life I wanted to create. I began living positively in earnest.

One of the things I did for practice was, when driving, I listened to two things only: *Secrets of the Millionaire Mind* by T. Harv Eker and *The Secret* audio book by Rhonda Byrne, thereby exposing me to the teachings of the master belief shifters currently living on the planet. I practiced everything I was learning about changing my beliefs and my mindset.

I was grateful every day for my dreams as if they were already manifested. Even though my current reality was not a match, I held pictures of that reality in my mind and positive thoughts and visions of being a millionaire.

Really? A millionaire? With the meager reality I was living? There's the rub. I had to *believe* that first it was possible – yes, of course, anything is possible to those that believe. Second, it was okay to have a big dream – yes, many of the people I was calling teacher said you must have a big dream! And third, take time everyday to focus on the life you really want so you have a goal to go towards and a vision to hold. You can't get what you want if you don't know what you want or your focus is on what you don't want.

It is important to imagine what you *want, need or desire* every day to get in and stay in the flow of positive thinking and positive focus. When I am what I call "in the flow," I feel like anything can happen. I believe everything is possible. After all, if it is possible for one it is possible for anyone.

My imagination is my workshop where my dreams are fashioned. I picture myself as already having achieved my dreams, seeing myself doing the things that I'll be doing when I've reached my goals. When I imagine my desires, I get my subconscious mind working toward making my mental pictures come true.

Shift Your Beliefs to Get What You Want

The first event I went to changed my life forever! It was T. Harv Eker's Millionaire Mind Intensive, a full three-day event designed to change your beliefs around money. Well, that is for me! I wanted to be a millionaire and I wanted to learn everything I could about the path to my freedom! On the final day we did an intense exercise during which we held a new belief in our hearts and minds as we went through the exercise. We had renovated our belief system for two transforming days leading up to this point.

This was the moment that changed my life.

As I moved through the exercise I said with full conviction and belief, "I can take care of myself!" while crying and laughing at the same time. My new belief was embedded.

I was really growing into a positive and happy person. Driving home from spending Christmas with family, I was looking for the least expensive gas I could find and kept searching as I was driving, finally ending up at a tiny gas station. Being alert has its rewards. While there, I saw a big poster — 'Holiday Millionaire Raffle. Would you like to be a millionaire?'

Why, yes, yes I would! Anything that had the word 'millionaire' in it got my attention. One of my affirmations was and still is,

When I have inspired thought, I act on it.

The moment came when I had the inspired thought to buy a ticket. I did not ask for, or pray to win the lottery, although you may. And, I never bought lottery tickets! This was a twenty-dollar ticket, so this would be a real stretch for me.

As I wondered, "Should I buy one of those tickets?" my dog started barking very excitedly and was jumping around

Conversations That Make a Difference

in the vehicle. I thought he had to go to the bathroom, so I quickly took him for a little walk. I thought it strange that he didn't even pee, he was just looking around. When he was back in the vehicle and I was ready to get in, I saw the sign again and I thought to myself, "Gee, before I leave I wonder if I should I get one of those tickets?" And, just as I had this thought, my dog started his barking again and jumping around in the window — and when I looked at him he was looking intensely right at me! Hmm.

I had a moment as I mentally tallied the balance in my checking account, as my history and old beliefs flooded me with lack thoughts. And then, in the blink of an eye, I shifted. After all, the sign on my dashboard was *When I have inspired thought, I act on it.* And, since my dog had never done this before, I smiled and thought, "There's my sign!"

It was three days before the drawing and when I asked the attendant if there were any tickets left he said, "Sure, how many do you want?" With a smile, I said to him, "Just one, and make it a winning one!" I could not choose the number I received because it was a statewide raffle and you got the next available number. I told myself that no matter the result this was a Christmas present to me. I kissed the ticket, held it in the air, gave thanks for winning and then tucked the ticket in my visor and forgot about it.

I had paid attention to the signs. I checked in with my intuition and when fear showed up I released the fear and I moved forward in faith and the belief that is was a good thing for me because I could feel a good feeling inside of me.

Well, the drawing came and went. A week after the drawing had taken place I finally remembered to look. There were twelve draws for a million dollars each as well as other money prizes. I started at the beginning looking at the winning numbers. On the twelfth and final draw for a million dollars I was startled. Those numbers looked familiar. Could it be? I hadn't looked at the ticket since I got it and it was still in the visor of my car.

At the time, I was on the phone with a friend and she sensed something and asked me what was wrong. Nothing! I told her I was just going to walk out to my car to check something. I printed out the numbers. I had to check a lottery ticket! I hustled on out to the car and pulled the ticket out of my visor. I gasped! "What's wrong?" I was asked again. Wait a minute, wait a minute... it looks like I won the lottery! "What?!!!!!"

Wait, wait. I painstakingly went over each and every single number to match it with what I had printed out. My mind did not believe it. I told my friend that I thought I had just won a million dollars. She screamed! I screamed! And it clicked! I shouted,

"I JUST WON A MILLION DOLLARS!!!!!"

Can you imagine how I felt? I laughed and danced around my yard for a long time repeating "Oh, my God! Oh, my God!" and "Thank you, thank you, thank you!" What would you do?

This story is not about winning a lottery raffle; it is about being in the *vibration of gratefulness that you already have what you want!* Believe it is so and it manifests. You can read the whole story in my book, *Shift Happens: How I Won a Million Dollars with the Law of Attraction* in which I give you a game plan on how to manifest your own dreams. www.CandiParker.com

You can be in dire straits and today you can begin to change your life — right now. To change your beliefs you have to THINK about it a lot, ACT as if you already have what you want and PRACTICE feeling grateful for having it. Put your FOCUS on what you *want*! Keep your ATTENTION on creating happiness. Maintain your positive thoughts and hold your vision with a grateful heart that it is already so. Be courageous and ready to be all that you are capable of being. Know in your heart that abundance and prosperity are indeed yours!

Because what you believe is what happens.

About the Author

Candi Parker is an Acupuncture Physician, certified Law of Attraction coach, book coach, publisher, bestselling author and Army veteran. As well as being a serial entrepreneur, she co-leads the Tallahassee chapter of the Women's Prosperity Network.

Through personal experience and extensive research, she has created an effective system for tapping into the multi-billion dollar industry of eBook sales with her course, *Write a Kindle Book in a Weekend.*

Her book, *Shift Happens: How I Won a Million Dollars with the Law of Attraction* is on Amazon in print and on Kindle.

The common theme in all Candi does is her passion and expertise in providing ways for people to achieve health, wealth and happiness.

www.CandiParker.com
www.PositiveTribe.com
www.ParkerHouseBooks.com

Conversations That Make a Difference

When I "Walked In" to My Life...
Everything Changed

Ariel Albani

I didn't know how to start. I kept hearing the voices of my angels saying, "Just write. Do it. It will all flow out." It is not the first time in my life I found myself given a task that I wasn't sure how to tackle. In the past, my immediate reaction would be to close down and not do it. To just settle for whatever was. But the day I chose to say *Yes* to allowing angels to speak through me, the day when I trusted in the angelic voice that told me I could, my life changed. I finally got on track with my life purpose. Let me tell you about how it unfolded for me.

You see, settling is easier to do but harder to live with. When you settle, you simply tell yourself over and over that you are happy where you are, while knowing deeply that this couldn't be farther from the truth. You wake up in the morning joyless, with no desire to seize the day, but rather focused on simply getting through it. You convince yourself that you can't really afford any changes. Sound familiar? You wonder how to find out your life purpose, and if you will ever have the chance to experience the "fulfillment" that you read about, which seems to constantly elude you. You settle for a life that is a bit uncomfortable, almost like a piece of clothing that you wear because it looks good according to others, but is not truly you and doesn't quite fit.

For many years I settled into a career that left me deeply unfulfilled. I was quite good at it. Yet the compliments that I received for my abilities to excel at work kept me paralyzed. I desperately wanted a life change but had no idea how to go about making that happen. I felt like fate must have chosen my work, my destiny, and my relationships, and I simply "dreamed" of a different reality without truly believing that it was possible. I was stuck.

The truth is that, when your heart says something and your actions are not congruent with your feelings, because you are too afraid to listen to your heart, you eventually get sick and you unconsciously invite chaos and crisis to manifest in your life. The chaos created by your rebellious soul that refuses to give up her dream, will turn your life into a rollercoaster that feels as if you are in a washing machine on spin. After some time in that cycle, you finally emerge a different and clearer person.

It was in the midst of a life crisis, when my health, my marriage, and my life in general fell apart, that life "kicked" me hard into action... and it hurt! Within a year, I found myself having to rebuild my life from scratch. This was to be the best gift life could have ever given me, but believe me when I tell you that it certainly did not feel like it at the time. As a person who does not like confrontation, I would rather have settled into a life of inconsequence and wishful thinking, instead of creating anything that would have invited the potential of criticism. Little did I know that a completely new awareness was about to begin!

After a year of despair, I found myself a single mom in a new country, facing choices. I wanted to change my life, and this was an opportunity to do that. I needed to renew my mind. I wanted a chance at living and finding my purpose. My thought process had to change.

I turned to yoga and the study of quantum physics. I became a seeker of truth and deeper understanding. As I opened myself to change, the miracles began to happen. I started taking classes: Reiki, hypnosis, spiritual guidance, and yoga. I embraced the goddess within me and worked through many layers of fears. You might have read this phrase before: "When the student is ready, the teacher will appear." I was ready and the most beautiful teachers appeared for me.

It was one summer day in July of 1998, after I had received my certification as a Reiki Master and had completed a year of yoga instruction and personal transformational sessions with one of my beloved teachers, when everything truly changed. I woke up a different person, the soul that had been, no longer was. I was a new person. I felt different. I was no longer the settling girl I had been. I was now A.R.I.E.L. I heard a loving voice within me clearly state, "Your name is **A R**eturn **I**nto **E**ternal **L**ove, Ariel." My first thought was one of excitement and glory; my second thought was, "How am I going to do this? What is this? I must have lost my mind!" Yet, the conviction in my heart about this new being that I now was far exceeded my doubts. I can't express in words the feeling, for it is only in the experience that you can tap into the depth of this awareness. I am guided to share this to assist you in embracing your own transformations, as "crazy" as they may seem.

Shift Your Beliefs to Get What You Want

I started by telling my family that from then on, they could call me Ariel; which incidentally is a man's name in my culture and that did not help! Their initial response was not too supportive. In retrospect, I am in awe that their love, support and acceptance ever happened, which indeed did, far beyond my expectations. I contacted a Unity minister and celebrated an "Ariel Baptism Celebration" with witnesses and beautiful chakra-colored candles. I felt so much joy! And lastly, I hired a lawyer, went to court and changed my name legally to Ariel. Yes, my conviction was very strong!

The first thing I noticed was that Ariel's thought process was very different from the old soul, "Rosanna." "Rosanna" had a very difficult time with every path and every decision, and was always ridden by fear. Ariel, on the other hand, was a super positive thinker! She was a natural at it and understood well that success comes from finding what gives you joy and allows you to be of service to others. She had the tools to create positive manifestations in the areas of health, relationships, finances, spiritual alignment and overall well-being. She was a born teacher, healing facilitator, artist, angel channel, and freelancer. She simply stood in love. My daughter fully embraced Ariel, and that enlightened my soul.

From that point of inspiration, I began to continue cultivating the gifts that Ariel brought with her as well as to understand more deeply the concept of a "walk in," which is when two souls share the same body in one incarnation. This happens by divine contract and is always for a higher good. Rosanna had completed her cycle and Ariel was needed upon Mother Earth. When a "walk in" occurs, the new soul completes the learning of the old before fully entering into her life purpose. This process can take years of deep learning, karmic release and consistent work towards self-realization. I spent ten years in the journey of transition before I felt whole as Ariel.

One of the greatest gifts I received was the mastering of the understanding of the Law of Attraction. This is a universal law that states that every thought carries a vibrational frequency and that frequency attracts frequencies similar to it. It works similarly to when you are seeking to find a radio station and you adjust the dial to the perfect frequency that allows you to listen to the kind of music you desire. Our thoughts carry vibrations, and every thought is a point of attraction. If your life is not as you would like it to be, examining your thought process, and learning how to change your thoughts to allow a different point of attraction, will change your life. It sounds so easy, yet it is a journey to get there!

Sometimes we have so many experiences in our life journey and perhaps thought processes we have inherited from our ancestors that it may take some life review and past life exploration to gain the necessary insights to help us change our thoughts. A deeper understanding of the higher purpose of our life experiences, particularly the most challenging ones, is often necessary to break through. As long as we feel confused and victimized by life, we are surrendering our divine right to manifest and be fully empowered! Superficially thinking positively is not enough to change our lives. We must trust, feel and believe our thoughts in order to effect change. This requires practice, and we may need a healing facilitator to assist us.

It took me time, discipline and diligence to change my thoughts, to embrace a life of service with great joy and love. The blessings that resulted have been well worth it. After continuing my education in the holistic approach to healing, and polishing the gifts Ariel brought as an angel channel, I left my hospitality career fully in 2002 to facilitate healing and awareness for others. It was a leap of faith that I took with courage. It involved giving up a steady income while I was a single mom. I believed the angelic guidance I felt. I was aware that my thoughts co-created a reality, and I knew that, if I was to be a teacher of the light, I had to walk in that light. I did it!

Since then my life has completely changed and continues to evolve every day. Through time I have witnessed hundreds of beautiful life transformations, and have helped others heal. I have witnessed new births heralded by the angels and have assisted souls in departing. My art was exhibited in a gallery in Dubai, and my healing work is now international. I have loved and lived fully in my power. My daughter has graduated from one of the best U.S. colleges. I have married my true love and have two very special young men as stepsons. My life is graced by my beloved animals and my very special little dog, Lolita Fairy. I am blessed with a loving and supportive family. My parents and my four sisters are my very best friends and loving supporters.

Being empowered in our truth and changing our thoughts does not mean that stressful life experiences disappear. It does mean that we are equipped and able to channel them in ways that build our lives and fuel our inspiration rather than weaken or destroy it.

I can't say that embracing a completely new thought process was easy. There were moments when fear knocked at my door, and yet every time Faith answered and found no one there. I learned to thrive with what is and my life has been a blessing to myself and others ever since. I am humbly grateful that I chose to change my thoughts and embrace the life that I was given. When I walked in to my life, everything changed. Perhaps it's time for you to step confidently into yours! Blessings!

About the Author

Ariel Albani is a seasoned certified wellness facilitator in the areas of yoga, meditation, Reiki, access consciousness bars, hypnosis, intuitive channeling and overall wellness. She is also an expressionist painter.

Ariel's work includes wellness workshops, transformational retreats and individual wellness sessions. She has taught yoga, Reiki and meditation internationally, most recently in Dubai, UAE and has been teaching Reiki certification courses for over 10 years.

Ariel holds a Bachelor of Arts Degree in Business Administration. Her further studies include Reiki Mastership, Yoga R.Y.T., Florida License in Massage Therapy, as well as Clinical Hypnosis, Access Consciousness Bars, Master Spirit Guide and Angel Card Reader Certifications. Ariel is member of the Holistic Chamber of Commerce in Orlando. She is fully bilingual in English and Spanish.

Ariel's work has been described as magical, ageless and spiritually beautiful.

To learn more about Ariel, visit: www.arielalbani.com

How I Lost My Mind and Found My Heart

Don Milton

At the age of fifteen, I was introduced to this poem, *If*, by Rudyard Kipling, at a time when I was totally entrenched in the traditional Catholic ways of my family. And although I was instantly quite enamored by the beauty of these words, never could I have imagined then just how profoundly and prophetically I would see my own life being unfolded between the lines of this poem!

> *If you can keep your head, when all about you*
> *Are losing theirs and blaming it on you;*
> *If you can trust yourself, when all men doubt you,*
> *But make allowance for their doubting too:*
> *If you can wait and not be tired by waiting,*
> *Or being lied about don't deal in lies,*
> *Or being hated, don't give way to hating,*
> *And yet don't look too good nor talk too wise;*

Life was all about financial security, good health, good fun and the right relationship. That's what I thought for a long time, well into my adulthood, when I was on the verge of financial security and in good health. I was married to the

Shift Your Beliefs to Get What You Want

same woman for sixteen years, we had two children and we were what people would call the perfect couple. If someone were looking at my life from the outside, they would see what most people in today's society would consider an almost picture perfect life.

In actuality, my wife and I were living a life of what I call comfortable misery, just surviving and living separate lives in the same home. Although, at the time, I had the IQ to qualify for Mensa, my EQ (emotional quotient) would not have even reached the baseline of the chart graph; I had none. So, much to the surprise of family and friends, we very sadly agreed to part ways. Even the attorneys couldn't believe how amicable our divorce was. During this time, financial security was on the horizon and yet that, too, ended - and with far less amicable results! After a change in real estate investment tax law tanked my business, I lived on my Keogh account, the home equity line, credit cards and money borrowed from friends.

An opportunity came to me that could potentially bring me financial security. I was to assist an investment group in putting a deal together that would yield me about half a million a year or more. That deal closed six months before my divorce in 1990. At the same time my marriage fell apart, I had my eye on the pot of gold that would keep filling itself yearly. Within the first year, I learned that the partners were dishonest, and the deal left me in even greater debt. I felt I was a good person and was a victim of other people's actions that led me to make poor decisions; leaving me feeling angry, frustrated and searching for answers.

I thought I'd be married for life. I thought I had this financial thing. Everything I thought life was about and was important to me had gone down the toilet. What the hell?

If you can dream - and not make dreams your master;
If you can think and not make thoughts your aim,
If you can meet with Triumph and Disaster
And treat those two impostors just the same;
If you can bear to hear the truth you've spoken
Twisted by knaves to make a trap for fools,
Or watch the things you gave your life to broken,
And stoop and build them up with worn out tools;

I've since discovered that it makes no difference how spiritual dis-ease manifests itself. It can be financial, it can be physical, it can be relational, and the bottom line is that everything that happens on the outside is a reflection of what is or isn't happening on the inside. The closer we come to living the life that our Spirit is here to live, the more congruent life will become. The outside always reflects the inside.

The road to spiritual wellness, which I've learned is the glue that holds our lives together and opens the doors to our heart and our dreams, was one that had a few turns in the road for me. I went from being religious, having been raised Catholic, to agnostic when I no longer believed in the heaven and hell of Catholicism, to finally finding my way to my own relationship with Spirit.

The way of ego is to have a plan and a back-up on top of a back-up plan. The way of Spirit is to take one step at a time and be in the moment. On my spiritual journey, I met a small group of people who I would study with, opening my mind just enough to allow my curiosity to be peaked for learning. Those people led me to Albert, a spiritual teacher I would work with when I wasn't looking for him; and the way our meeting happened was clearly divinely orchestrated. With

Shift Your Beliefs to Get What You Want

Albert, as a result of studying with him in Sedona for a week and for ninety days after that, I learned to use journaling, meditating, prayer, reading inspirational books and using the 12 Steps as tools to open my heart and to be there in support of others as they learned to do the same. Those tools kept me walking the path that Spirit was leading me on.

Let's face it; most of us are not able to do this alone. On my own, I would not have found the 12 step meetings, since there was nothing that would have otherwise led me to the steps. Also, I would not have prayed; it was not something that had ever worked for me in the past. Putting the combination of the four tools together is what sparked the shift within me. With Albert's guidance, and my willingness to follow direction while trusting the process, I got extraordinary results. I learned through this experience, that it's all about trusting someone, trusting the process and trusting Spirit.

The most profound event occurred just before the ninety days of my work with Albert came to a close. During a prayerful moment on my knees at the side of my bed, I felt for the first time in my life, the immense power and loving presence of God! From that point on, the only prayer that has meant anything to me is my asking God to give me the direction I need to know what I am supposed to do today, the Faith and Courage to do it and the ability to not be attached to the results.

The process took several years for me to begin trusting Spirit in my personal life. At the same time, there was such a huge disconnect between personal and business for me. I didn't think there was a place for spirituality in my business. When I was able to let go of the layers of fear that kept me from being in alignment in every area of my life, as I could clearly see I was being guided to do, everything came together. I had to be willing to be embarrassed, look foolish, spend money and ask for money. I had to be willing to do whatever was before me to do. It was through taking baby steps of building trust and letting go of the fear that I am able to live in Spirit in all aspects of my life today.

> *If you can make one heap of all your winnings*
> *And risk it on one turn of pitch-and-toss,*
> *And lose, and start again at your beginnings,*
> *And never breathe a word about your loss;*
> *If you can force your heart and nerve and sinew*
> *To serve your turn long after they are gone,*
> *And so hold on when there is nothing in you*
> *Except the Will, which says to them, "Hold on!"*

My experience over the past twenty-four years has led me to know that there is a Cycle of Creation determining how our lives go. The cycle seems to be that our beliefs determine our thoughts, which determine our feelings, which determine our actions, which determine our results. Ultimately, our results reinforce our beliefs. This runs 24/7, mostly in our subconscious so that we are not even aware of why we are doing what we are doing. We just think that we are consciously running our lives. The good news is that every healthy belief we have makes our life easy without much effort. The bad news is that every unhealthy belief that we have makes things very difficult and prevents us from making much change using discipline, will power and intentions.

The work that I do today as an emotional freedom coach allows me to quickly assist a person to identify their

Shift Your Beliefs to Get What You Want

dysfunctional beliefs, clear them and install healthier beliefs in a manner that can dramatically change one's life for the better without years of agony and struggle. Even though I would never have consciously chosen to experience some of the horrendous things that have occurred in my life over the years, I would not exchange the lessons that I have learned for elimination of the experiences.

If I tune in and my guidance says, "This doesn't feel like it's going to make my heart sing," then the answer is no. So for me, it's been more of a process of living from the heart instead of just talking it. It's all about the inner work, the inner life. What's going to manifest on the outside is not going to be any more valuable or solid or real than where it's coming from; the inside. It's interesting that I'm doing the work that I do now. I'm a guy who helps people connect with their heart, value their emotions and clear those emotions that hold people back from their best life. Imagine that... This coming from someone who's EQ was as low as Forrest Gump's IQ.

If you can talk with crowds and keep your virtue,
Or walk with kings - nor lose the common touch,
If neither foes nor loving friends can hurt you,
If all men count with you, but none too much:
If you can fill the unforgiving minute
With sixty seconds worth of distance run,
Yours is the Earth and everything that's in it,
And - which is more - you'll be a Man my Son!

This poem continues to resonate with me and has become even more meaningful, beautiful and personal, as my shift in belief has brought me to a complete shift in my life. As the doors opened, I trusted, and as the information became available, I learned. I followed my heart to the life I was always meant to live. I'm following the yellow brick road.

I invite you to begin your path by taking a step, an action step to connect with me or one of the authors in this book, who you resonate with. Just reading it is not enough. There has to be some daily practice in place in order to go deeper and move further along your path. I encourage you to listen for the voice of Spirit in your life, take direction from a mentor and walk, one step at a time, one day at a time toward a better life; one that you are totally in control of. Break free of the bondage of this world; be in the world but not of the world. Live your life as one of Peace, Love and Joy.

About the Author

Don Milton is available for a limited number of private sessions each week by phone, Skype, or in-person and prefers to do these with folks who choose to do his twelve-week life transformational program and will do single sessions as needed. He can also do group work by phone or in-person and these programs are scheduled as needed and generally initiated by someone who wants their group to be exposed to his work in a more economically affordable manner. Don has also created a series of DIY EFT videos showing how to use basic EFT for seventeen different issues for those who would like to have this experience at a nominal cost in the comfort of their own home. He also has a fun site about his cookbook with videos showing most of the recipes in process.

www.donmilton.net
www.eftvideotutorials.com
www.cookingwithheartenergy.com
don@donmilton.net
Skype: growthbydesign
Phone: 205.822.5962

From Pieces to Peace - Three Minutes at a Time

Dina Proctor

Just over five years ago I hit the rock bottom point in my life. I didn't want to live anymore. I felt like I had a gaping, painfully desolate black hole inside of myself that no matter what I tried, I couldn't fill. I was clinically depressed, hopelessly addicted to alcohol and food, and money, and men, among other things, and had tried to fix myself in too many ways to count over the prior ten years.

During my twenties I struggled with clinical depression. In addition to trying therapy and anti-depressants, I thought if I could just manifest the perfect boyfriend, the perfect job, the perfect body, that I would feel better. I moved apartments. I changed cities. I upgraded my boyfriends. I went on diets, I tried cleanses, I went off sugar, I went back on sugar, I gave up meat, I ate meat, I went high-protein, I went high-carb. You name it, I tried it.

And the self-help books. Oh, the self-help books! My shelves were lined with them. I would read a little of each one, but never had the motivation to immerse myself in their get-happy-quick tips, so nothing ever changed. Months and years wore on while my depression worsened and the black hole inside me continued to expand.

Shift Your Beliefs to Get What You Want

After almost ten years of all of this work: the incessant changes, the medications, the cleanses, the jobs, the boyfriends, the cars, I finally discovered something that really worked; something that made me feel better than almost anything; that gave me confidence and made me feel attractive for the first time in my life. This magical solution was alcohol.

As my drinking increased, my concern about the moral fiber of my character decreased. I was becoming someone I didn't recognize. I was stealing money, lying to my friends, waking up next to men I had just met, and drinking at work. I reached a point after over two years of constant alcohol in my bloodstream where I could no longer live with who I had become. That's the day I began to plan to take my own life.

One Sunday evening in the fall of 2008 I decided on the following Saturday to be the day I would end it. I'd give myself that week to get everything together at home and at work before I left this world for good. I would put myself out of my misery; not because I wanted to die, but because I had tried everything I could think of to make me want to live and nothing was working. I hated myself, my life, and just about everything about just about everything.

But on that Sunday night I was in such inner emotional agony that I didn't think I could make it even six more days to fulfill my plan. I needed to feel better, and I had to make it one more week to make sure everything that I would leave behind was in order, but how? Then an idea occurred to me. It might make me feel better to see how bad it might have been – to see what folks whose lives were worse than mine looked like. I was living down the street from an addiction recovery center and thought if I could anonymously go and get a glimpse of some of those folks I might feel better about myself, my drinking, and the bad person I'd become.

So I went. They had open meetings for the community to join so I sat in the very back row and listened to the people speaking at the front of the room, telling their stories. And then, completely unexpectedly, I began crying.

Denial is very common among those of us, currently or previously, in the throes of addiction. And what came as a complete surprise to me was the realization that my life was *worse* than some of the stories I was hearing. Only one bottle of wine a night? Please. Stopping to get help before you started stealing and waking up next to people you had only known for three hours? Really? How on earth could these honest people belong here and yet I thought I didn't?

This realization was the beginning of my awakening. And those tears were the very, very tender beginning of my own healing. I stuck around the program because it felt good to be there, but I didn't commit to living by its teachings or to quit drinking for that matter, for almost three months. I was too busy postponing my suicide one day at a time. I kept telling myself *you don't have to kill yourself today; you can always do it tomorrow.* The people at the recovery center focused on not drinking one day at a time. I focused on staying a member of the human population one day at a time.

Then one day at a meeting, I heard a certain woman speak. I'll call her Grace, because that is the essence of what she exuded and that's also what she became to me; my saving Grace. She sat in front of this big room of over fifty people in her designer skinny jeans with her cute little haircut, all put together and perfect, talking about how her heroin addiction had led her down more horrific paths than alcohol had taken me.

Shift Your Beliefs to Get What You Want

I could not believe that the woman she was describing was one and the same with the woman telling this story – she was so pretty and confident and warm and honest. I was so drawn to her that I went up to her after the meeting and asked for her phone number. We met for coffee and she told me how she did it – how she climbed out of hell and into an amazing life she had never known possible. I told her I wanted that too and she said she would help me, talk to me every single day, and teach me the way.

Grace was a tough-love kind of mentor. She didn't fall for any of my sweet-talk or excuses. She would tell me, "If you want what I have, you have to do the work." And it turned out the first of this "work" was to learn to meditate.

At first I balked at her suggestion. *Meditate?* What exactly does that mean – and more importantly – how on earth is sitting there in a floaty, wistful way going to help with any of this self-hatred and suicidal obsession I was stuck in? How would that take away this intense physical and emotional compulsion to drink constantly? I balked at her suggestion. But she seemed to expect that.

Grace's response to me was, "If your way was working you wouldn't be here with me right now, you'd be off living your life happily ever after. But here you are, so why don't you try my way for a while?"

Well now, that was a good point. I agreed to try it her way.

Grace's first meditation instruction was to sit still every morning and focus on my breathing for twenty minutes. How hard could that be?

The first morning I set a timer and settled in for my twenty minutes. But after about thirty seconds the craving to drink overwhelmed me, and negative thoughts about suicide and self-hatred flared up strongly. I forced myself to endure the inner agony and sit as still as I could as I focused on my breathing. But after only about three minutes, my skin was crawling, I was shaking and sweating uncontrollably, and I physically could not sit still any longer. So I got up, cried a little, and slowly, painfully went about my day.

A couple of hours later it nagged at me that I hadn't completed the entire twenty minutes as Grace had instructed. So I tried to sit down again, setting the timer, and using all of my effort to try and focus on my breathing.

Predictably, after about three minutes the experience again became intolerable and – not being able to stand it any longer — I ended the meditation.

Day after day this went on. Three minutes here, three minutes there. Three minutes was my limit. I thought Grace would be disappointed in my failure to follow her directions, but she was surprisingly encouraging, telling me whatever I was capable of doing was great.

About eight weeks of this messy three-minutes-at-a-time meditation practice, something unexpected happened. I came out of one of my three-minute meditations and even though I was in my same old apartment, nothing about it was "same old" to me.

I opened my eyes and looked around the room, noticing my everyday things as if for the first time. The wooden furniture, the candles, and especially my cat, had a special glow about them. My vision was different; I felt like I had switched into a 3-D movie way of seeing the world. And when I got up from my seated meditation I noticed that my conscious awareness was several feet above and slightly behind my body. I was acutely aware that this higher vantage point was actually where the "real me" was all the time – above my physical self, always present but never accessed.

Shift Your Beliefs to Get What You Want

How could I have never known this? These physical bodies are like little finger-puppets we animate to navigate the physical world, but that our true essence, the "puppeteer" is actually much, much bigger than our small bodies?

I stayed in this state of hovering above my body for about three days. For this entire time period I had absolutely no mind chatter. I had never even known that was possible! No negative thoughts. Not a single one. And I fell in love with everyone I met – not in the "love" like I did with guys when I was drunk at bars, but true, honest, real appreciation and connection with every single person's soul essence. I became capable of extended eye contact and long silences. I saw the personalities of trees and flowers (who knew? They have souls and intentions too!), the innermost essence of love within and throughout every single living being.

From this state it was plain to me that anything I wanted in the physical world could be found by focusing on it from this larger, higher state of being. The physical world is merely a mirror, a reflection, of the depth of the connection between the "little me" (my physical self) and the "big me" (my soul-essence self). Knowing this connection exists and keeping it prominent in my life became my number one priority.

And then my life started to evolve--big time. I stayed with Grace through the recovery program. I made amends for stealing, I repaired relationships with people I'd hurt, completely re-vamped my close relationships, healed from addiction, and lost the weight I'd gained after my drinking addiction became an eating addiction. Every single thing I wanted to do I found in my three-minute meditations first.

I learned that instead of money or a lover, I'd actually been seeking empowerment all those years; the true connection to my inner source of power, peace, and wisdom. I'd been plugging into all of these other things seeking satisfaction, but they never quite fit right and I'd always needed more and more...and more. But this higher-self connection was amazingly and deeply fulfilling in a way I'd never experience before.

Those three days of serenity, my work with Grace, and my willingness to face my demons and heal, changed – and saved — my life.

Today, I use my peace to help other people find theirs. I teach what I call 3x3 Meditation - three minutes, three times a day. I love speaking to groups, working with people one-on-one and co-creating with people who are experts in wellness methods, to share the message that no matter where you are, what you've done, who you think you've become, you can always find a way to heal and finally find that elusive inner peace.

About the Author

Dina Proctor is a life and business coach, inspirational speaker, and best-selling author of *Madly Chasing Peace: How I Went From Hell to Happy in Nine Minutes a Day*. After hitting emotional rock-bottom, she quite unintentionally created a process called 3x3 Meditation (3 minutes, 3 times a day) that enabled her to transform every aspect of her life. From weight loss and banishing addictive cravings to reconstructing relationships, this simple and yet incredibly effective method has gained the support of Jack Canfield and Dr. Bruce Lipton, and is now helping thousands of others around the world improve their lives. Connect with Dina at www.madlychasingpeace.com

The Gift of Gratitude

Teresa Velardi

Gratitude is the key that unlocks the door to prosperity in all areas of your life.

What do you mean you have nothing to be grateful for? Seriously? What about the beautiful children you brought into this world? And the grandchildren they gifted you with? What about the fact that every few seconds without you even realizing it, your lungs take in life giving air so you can live another moment? How about the roof over your head and the man who loves you? Who else would do *anything* for you? Shall I go on? You have nothing to be grateful for? Really?

That was a my response when I asked someone very close to me to stop the ranting about all that was wrong and all that she didn't have. I asked her to stop yelling, sit down and tell me three things she was grateful for. How about just one? Her response? "I have nothing to be grateful for!" You might as well have knocked me over with a feather. Instead, in between just a couple of those breaths that give life, came the list of whatever I could think of off the top of my head that I knew was part of her life. Most of which I, myself, am grateful for.

Every time I think of that moment, two thoughts come to mind: "Thank God that's not me today," is the first. "Thank you God I have shifted my attitude to be one of gratitude," is the second. Honestly, I feel sad and sorry for people who are living with ungrateful hearts. It's a sad and lonely place to be. It's a place of constant and consistent despair. It feels like nothing will ever go right, and even if it does, it's only temporary. The ungrateful heart believes that there will never be enough, they can never have enough, no one will ever do enough for them, and they will never be able to do enough for themselves. There will never be enough money; they will never have a chance to live a good life. It's upsetting to even think of living a life like that ever again.

I can honestly say that because at one time in my life, I was one of those people who had an ungrateful heart. I was so wrapped up in my sorrow, my sadness and my out of control life that I simply could not focus on what I was grateful for. I couldn't get my mind off of the things that weren't working and I completely lost sight of anything that was working. I couldn't see the forest through the trees so to speak. I couldn't see all that I had in my life because I was focused on what I didn't have. I didn't know what living gratefully was.

When we are caught up in our "stuff", the things that keep us stuck, we tend to forget all the good things that are happening around us, the people who make a difference in our lives and the things we have been blessed with. We forget to say "thank you," and lose sight of what is right before our eyes to be grateful for. We lose touch with those people who love us unconditionally; they love us for who we are not what we have or what we can do. We forget that we *have* more than most people around the world, even when times are difficult. We tend to take things for granted. Somehow, we just expect it all. Where is the gratitude? How did we become such blind and selfish people?

> *"The more you recognize and express gratitude for the things you have, the more things you will have to express gratitude for."* ~ Zig Ziglar

If only we could stop and consciously breathe in the beauty of the sunrise, or the sunset while gratitude filled our hearts that we have eyes to see it. We can. It is in the things that we take for granted that we find our way to shift our attitude to one of gratitude.

For me, I had to write it all down. I had to make a list of the things I was grateful for. It was the only way I could get through the pain of the life I was living. I began with one thing every day. Then it became two and then three; and before I knew it, I was questioning how I could have missed all the beauty and wonder that was around me. I gave thanks for a little and I found a lot more to be thankful for. One day at a time I made my list. It's something that I have continued to do daily. I write down at least three things or people I am grateful for every day. It's the first thing I do in the morning and the last thing I do at night. I've made gratitude a habit. Since I have been engaged in this process, I've found that I usually don't worry, and I have more confidence in general.

Gratitude is a mindset, an attitude; a shift in belief from "there's not enough" to "there's more than enough." It's like flipping a switch from negative thinking to positive thinking and from lack to abundance.

Shift Your Beliefs to Get What You Want

"If the only prayer you ever said was 'thank you,' that would be enough." ~ Meister Eckhart

For years, I would bargain with God. "Please God; if you make my husband stop drinking I'll never say another bad thing about him or anyone else." Or "Please God, if you help me earn enough money for those new shoes, I'll put extra money in the basket at church." How about this prayer, I'm sure you've prayed a similar one to this: "Lord, please let me earn enough money before they turn off the lights, or the water, or the gas in my house." I promise this, I'll do that, I'll never do this, I'll always do that. I need, I want, are all prayers of lack mindset. I heard someone say that many people think that God is this huge vending machine in the sky and whenever we ask for something, it will show up. To some degree that's true, but I don't think bargaining is the way to get what we want. I think it's the shift in belief, the shift in focus that brings more into our lives. I believe that God wants us to have all that we desire. I also believe that we have to have the hearts for those things and the responsibility to be able to receive and live with them.

How do we pray prayers of abundance? It's the gift of gratitude.

A prayer of Gratitude is the one thing; at least it's the one thing I have found, that will bring more into our lives. The practice of gratitude, feeling it and acknowledging it in some way, breeds more to be grateful for. Prayers of gratitude for what we have now and for what we anticipate we will have in the future are the way of the grateful heart. The key is, however, you have to feel the gratitude. Bob Proctor teaches that you project the gratitude for something by using these words: "I am so happy and grateful now that _____."

Conversations That Make a Difference

You fill in the blank to create a gratitude prayer or affirmation. For example, I am so happy and grateful now that each day is filled with love, joy, inspiration and peace. Or I'm so happy and grateful now that I am financially free. Do you see how the prayers of gratitude differ from the laundry list of bargaining chips?

Prayer from a perspective of gratitude and abundance brings more of the same; more to be grateful for and more abundance. Prayers of lack and pleading for something to be fixed or paid give more power to that mindset of there not being enough. What you focus on expands. It is your choice what you will focus on.

I find it interesting that people who never feel as though they have enough, never ever do. Even when they have enough, in *their* minds, it will never be enough because the mindset they live with is one of lack instead of abundance.

Have you ever noticed that people who have much usually add to their abundant lives? I'm remembering the words "what you think about, you bring about." People who live from grateful hearts live abundant lives. Contrary to what most people believe, abundance is not only in finances. It's also in relationships, physical health and wellbeing, spiritual wellbeing, and emotional wellbeing. It all stems from a grateful heart, and an abundance mindset.

"Piglet noticed that even though he had a Very Small Heart, it could hold a rather large amount of Gratitude."
~ A. A. Milne, Winnie-the-Pooh

It's been my experience that gratitude fills your heart so completely that there isn't room to want for anything more. That's not to say that we won't, of course we will want more.

Shift Your Beliefs to Get What You Want

The difference is, we appreciate all that we have so our hearts are full. With a daily practice of thanksgiving, or gratitude, we recognize that our hearts can hold more than we ever imagined. We think our hearts are full, until we realize that we have something else to be grateful for. It is a perpetual process. There is always room for more. Grateful hearts are always open, full and ready to give and receive more.

There is so much to be grateful for around us, within us, before us and behind us. All we have to do is open our eyes and our hearts to see and feel it.

I invite you to begin a daily practice that will bring awareness to what you have to be grateful for. Watch your life change and flourish when you are open to receiving the gift of gratitude.

As we express our gratitude, we must never forget that the highest appreciation is not to utter words, but to live by them.
~ John F. Kennedy

You can express your gratitude daily on line at http://bitly.com/gratefulhearts

About the Author

Teresa Velardi is an Author, Speaker, Potter and Transformational Life Coach.

She will take you on "Your Personal Transformational Journey", using pottery as an illustration for your own transformation from a ball of clay to a work of art! Along the way, you will learn how to unleash your power while connecting with your creative gifts and talents to live your most authentic life. Bring out the greatness within you as you discover that you already have the ability to shift every aspect of your life into high gear! Uncover your Dynamic Woman within and Wake Up to your most powerful, prosperous and passionate life.

Learn more about Teresa at
www.teresavelardi.com
www.wakeupwomen.com
www.transformationaltuesdays.com
www.dynamicwomenlive.com
email: teresavelardi@gmail.com

There's Another Way of Looking at This Seeing From a Higher Perspective

Judee Light

Every day is a new day; every moment is a new moment. And if you have things in your life that aren't feeling good, you can choose again . . . you can choose to look at them differently. You have the power to shift your perception, shift your belief. Really! And in doing so, you shift your reality.

I used to think that I saw *reality* in my life, and that reality was a *fact*! And that was just the way it was. *Not!* I have learned that I can create a new reality for myself by shifting my perceptions.

Years ago, I learned that we don't see things as they *are*, we see them as we *perceive* them to be. And the way we have been conditioned in the past often keeps us from seeing all there is to see. We actually have blind spots . . . until we learn to see differently.

I have found that sharing ways I have chosen to look at things differently over the years (that brought me amazingly positive results) has inspired others to make similar shifts. Some of my shifts I learned from wonderful teachers, and some were aha's that came out of the blue! (Someone once told me that "out of the blue" was a code word for God.)

One of the most significant shifts I made was as a result of what I learned from Lou Tice of *The Pacific Institute*. There was a time when I would not go for something I wanted if I didn't know how to get it, or did not have the resources I thought I needed (money, knowledge, skills, abilities, etc.). I believed I had to get the necessary knowledge or resources *before* I could go for the goal. Lou Tice taught me the psychology of how affirmations, visualization, and feelings work — how the brain works and how the creative process works. With a better understanding of this process, I saw that my job is to hold the vision, keep my attention on it, and feel what it would feel like to have that as a reality. The "how to" is then created by my Creative Subconscious Mind. To see this play out was amazing! Almost like magic at times.

Another teacher, Edwene Gaines, confirmed this when she taught me that the "how to" is God's business, not my business. Wow! No longer did I stop myself from going for goals because I didn't know *how* to get them. The "how to" was no longer relevant!

This change in belief so empowered me that I quit my job seven years short of full retirement (I *had* to do it! I could no longer stay in a job that dragged me down, just for the money.) Many people thought I was crazy! I decided to make a shift in perception right then and there about *crazy*. I looked up *crazy* in the dictionary and came up with my favorite definitions: *extraordinary* and *unbound* (free). Yes, I was crazy!

I stopped saying "I quit my job" and changed it to "I graduated from my job." This shift uplifted me. When we graduate in school, we have learned a lot, had a lot of great experiences, and it's time to move up to a higher level. That's what I did! I took a leap of faith and went out on my own as an independent contractor. I have never regretted my decision. On the contrary, I am forever grateful for graduating myself from that job.

Then it came to me that, instead of being twice divorced, I had graduated from two marriages! Instead of looking at divorce as a failure, I could see it as a completion and a transition in moving forward. Yes!

By now, you may have noticed that I like to look on the bright side — of people, situations, and things. For years, I have made it a practice to look at things differently if my first perception does not feel good. I learned that there is always another way to look at something...and another, and another, and another...

I want to share with you some of the shifts in perceptions and beliefs I have made over the years that have served me well, and continue to serve me well. I first give you the old ways of perceiving, that gave me negative, heavy feelings, or vibrations, and then the *new ways* I choose to look at the things or situations that give me positive, lighter feelings, or vibrations:

Old way of seeing and languaging . . . *New way of seeing and languaging*

Problem . . . *Opportunity for growth.*

Failure. . .*Resting place between successes, learning experience. I simply didn't get the result I wanted (so on to Plan B or C, and so on!)*

Conversations That Make a Difference

Try . . . *Intend.*

I don't know . . . *I know I can find out. There is an answer. All the answers are inside me.*

No way! . . . *Way! There's always a way. I just don't see it yet.*

I've been betrayed . . . *I'm being called to a higher level of consciousness.*

Feeling fear . . . *I use fear as a reminder that I'm focusing my attention on what I* don't *want...so when I feel fear come up, it is my signal to think about what I want instead of what I don't want!*

Feeling pain, anger, sadness, fear . . . *I'm feeling energy. I bless this energy and use it to get clear on what I want and to fuel my dreams! I can use this energy to get into action.*

Deadline . . . *Finish line, target date.*

Feeling discomfort . . . *Here I grow again — I'm expanding my comfort zone!* (We always feel discomfort when we are expanding our comfort zone — growing — and when we know this is simply part of the process, we can celebrate it as a sign of growth.)

Chaos, confusion . . . *Transformation time! Breakthrough is almost here!* (All living organisms go

Shift Your Beliefs to Get What You Want

through chaos in the process of transforming to a higher level. When we know that chaos is simply part of the transformation process, we can celebrate our upcoming transformation to a higher level.)

Darkness . . . *The dawn is almost here! Yay!*

Roadblocks, obstacles . . . *Stepping stones to something better.*

I'm losing it . . . *I've mastered the level I was on, and now I am at the beginning of the next level!* (Using the school analogy again, when we move up a grade, we have mastered the last one, and we are a beginner at the next level, which can feel confusing or overwhelming at first. Yet soon we are mastering the new level, and we continue to move up.)

I feel like I am going backwards! . . . *I'm really backing up for a running leap forward!*

My life is falling apart! . . . *In truth, my life is coming together in a new way, at a higher level!*

I'm on the verge of . . . *I'm in the process of* (For example, when you say, "I am on the verge of a breakthrough," you are still holding yourself apart from it. Yet, when you say, "I am in the process of a breakthrough," you are in it and it will soon be completed!)

Stepchild, stepfather, stepmother . . . *Bonus child, bonus father, bonus mother* (I got this from Susan Sarandon and Tim Robbins when they were on *Oprah* talking about blending their families.)

    These are just a few examples of ways I learned to shift into more positive ways of seeing and being, which then make me a powerful magnet that attracts my good in the most wonderful ways!

    When you start looking on the bright side, be prepared for some people to say, "You need to be realistic!" You can simply say, "Thank you for sharing that. However, you are talking about historical reality — the past. I am creating a new reality!"

    And, some people may call you crazy when you start making these kinds of shifts. This is when you can remember my two favorite definitions of *crazy* — *unbound* and *extraordinary*! I encourage you to get a little crazy — and have fun with your new ways of seeing!

About the Author

Judee Light is a speaker, teacher, author, editor, mentor, and facilitator. She is the owner of Feeling Uplifted Now (F.U.N.) www.FeelingUpliftedNow.com

She inspires people to move beyond the perceived safety of their comfort zones to connect with their passion and go for their dreams. She facilitates them in improving the quality of their lives through improving the quality of their thoughts and their language. She offers teleclasses, GrowShops, PlayShops, and one-on-one Walk & Talk sessions.

Because it is challenging to expand your personal growth when you are not healthy or are in pain, Judee also facilitates others in enhancing their health and well-being through natural products:

PowerStrips™ for pain relief
http://judeelight.FGXpress.com,
and SolarStrips™ for nutrition:
http://judeelight.mySolarStrips.com.

Judee is Co-leader of the Tallahassee Chapter, Women's Prosperity Network http://WPNGlobal.com/Tallahassee

Conversations That Make a Difference

You Don't Have To See It to Believe It

Sandra Champlain

L ook around you. What do you see? Yes, I am talking to you, the person reading these words. Would you be willing to play with me for just a moment? Stop reading, glance up, what you see? Pay attention to some of the things you see around you right now.

As I sit in my living room writing this, I see my laptop, the television, my coffee table and the remote control. There are many books and pictures; through the windows I see cars passing by and lush, green trees gently swaying in the breeze. What do you see?

Let's both take a moment to listen. I hear birds singing and cars traveling by. I hear a clicking sound with every button I press on my keyboard. Somewhere far away is the sound of a lawnmower. What do you hear?

Direct your attention now to the thoughts in your head and the sensations in your body. I am going on a big trip tomorrow and there are so many things I need to accomplish before I depart. I am worried that there won't be enough time to do all the things I need to do. My mind is preoccupied with my future plans and tension fills my body. My fingertips

Shift Your Beliefs to Get What You Want

are tingly, my heart feels like it is racing, I'm only taking short breaths and my skin feels a bit cold. What about you? What thoughts are going on in your mind as you read this? How does your body feel right now? Take a minute and really feel what it feels like to be in your skin.

In this world we live in, everything seems so real, doesn't it? We know things are real because we can see, touch, smell, hear and taste them. However, what if I told you that the things we think are real could very well be illusions? Would the thoughts in your head tell you that I am crazy? What if I told you that the thought you just had might not be real either? What if I told you that around you right now, there is a very real, invisible world, filled with activity? Would you believe me?

The name of this book is *Shift Your Beliefs to Get What You Want.* The title implies that the results we currently have in our lives are because of our current beliefs. My dad used to say, "Sandra, if you think you can or think you can't...you are right!" Our current beliefs lead to our thoughts which lead to our actions which lead to our results. Let me share with you an example. A good friend of mine was laughed at as a child while drawing a picture of a horse. She created the belief that "I'm not good at art" and stopped being artistic. As an adult she had an opportunity to paint a picture, for fun. A professional artist took one look at her painting and knew right away, she was a genuine, gifted artist. In that moment her belief changed and her future opened up to doing what she always loved to do...creating artwork!

My intention with this chapter is to help you shift your beliefs. However, in order for a shift to occur, you must be willing and be open to the possibility that something really good might come out of it! You may not be open and that is ok, too. You may be reading this chapter from a "you'll have to convince me" attitude. It's neither good nor bad. Stick with the same beliefs you've always had, you'll think the same thoughts you usually do, take your normal daily actions and ultimately have the same results that you have right now. This is perfectly fine. You've made it this far and you will continue in the future. I do think you are ready for something new. You know how I know that? You took the first step and are reading this book!

Let's go back in time. Did you know that at one time the people living on Planet Earth believed that the world was flat? Seems ridiculous now, but pretend for a moment that you believed it. What would your life be like today? You probably wouldn't venture too far from home and you wouldn't take a cruise for fear of falling off the edge of the earth! Life would be okay, because you wouldn't know that there could be any other way to live. However, if you believe, instead that the world is round, what kind of adventures and joy could you have? I've enjoyed the beaches of Mexico, the roller coasters in Florida, the neon lights in Las Vegas and the giant parties of Oktoberfest in Germany. New worlds open up when our beliefs change!

What beliefs do you have about yourself? You may be like me; I am prone to some pretty negative self-talk. When I woke up this morning, I hit the snooze button on the alarm clock several times and stayed cuddled under my covers. I did not want to face the day and the responsibilities. What's happened to young Sandra, who thought life was an adventure and didn't like naps or going to bed early? Children often spring out of bed in the morning ready to start their day!

Shift Your Beliefs to Get What You Want

As adults we not only dread getting out of bed, but we hate what we see when look in the mirror. Most of us have plenty of things we do not like about ourselves. What are your first thoughts when you look in the mirror? Do you have a bathroom scale that can make or break your day? Now, think of the judgments you have about yourself. Do you think you are smart, gorgeous, confident and successful? Or do you start the day feeling not good enough, unattractive, unlovable and afraid? Do you feel like you have failed many, many times?

Belief Shift #1

You are NOT the person your negative self-talk tells you that you are and I can prove it! Ask six people in your life that know you well, what words they would use to describe you. If you don't have people readily available to ask, you can still do the exercise.

Get a piece of paper and write their names across the top. Under each name, write the words that person would use to describe you. Be honest. How does that person think of you? Jot down as many words as you can. Look at the piece of paper in front of you. Compare those words with the words you spoke to yourself in the negative self-talk you did this morning. Notice anything peculiar? Here are my results: as much as I want to beat up on myself that I am not good enough, lazy, unattractive, unlovable and I think I am a failure, the words on my page showed something entirely different. The six people closest to me would say things like "Sandra is a hard-worker, reliable, loving, fun, compassionate, smart, beautiful, kind, inspiring and successful."

Isn't it funny that people in our lives see us one way and we see ourselves another way? Who is right? Here is some great news: your friends are right! You are incredible and I am too. Imagine a game of tug-of-war. You are the only one pulling strongly that you are stupid, a failure, uncoordinated, and that you don't matter to others. Six people on the other side of the rope are calling you brilliant, special, caring, fun to be with and powerful. Basically, our loved ones are correct about us, we are great people. What would be possible in your life if your actions correlated with a person who truly believed all those positive things about themselves and didn't listen to negative self-talk? I encourage you to think about how your life would look, what actions you would take and what results would you have. Would we hit the snooze button if we believed we are each awesome people and that something miraculous would be or could be happening at any minute today? I think we'd spring out of bed ready for the adventure!

Belief Shift #2
Look up again at all those things you see around you. Each thing is made up of what we call 'matter.' Inside matter there are things called molecules and inside of molecules there are things called atoms. Here is the cool part: if we were to put a tiny camera inside one of the atoms making up your hand, for example, the camera would not see anything! There is no 'matter' inside the atoms that make up 'matter.' The inside of an atom simply contains ENERGY bouncing around. Your hand is actually made up of invisible vibrating energy. Everything you can see, touch, smell, taste or hear is simply vibrating energy, including YOU.

Remember the invisible world I mentioned earlier? It is simply not true that we must see something to believe it is real. Can you see the wireless internet signal that connects your cell phone or laptop to the internet? Can you see the GPS signal that seems to magically know exactly where you are? Can you see the radio waves that find your car allowing you to listen to music while driving? Imagine a couple of hundred years ago telling one of our ancestors that someday there will be a small box in a "horseless carriage" that would allow them to hear music and voices. They wouldn't have believed you, would they? However, when it was possible to transmit and receive radio waves, a whole, new world became available. Once again, a belief changed and new, incredible results followed. I could not imagine a world without all of this incredible technology!

Belief Shift #3

In my book *We Don't Die - A Skeptic's Discovery of Life After Death*, I share my belief that our bodies will disappear at death but we do not. We simply change form, like a log that has burned and turned into heat, or a puddle of water that has turned to moisture. I believe we continue to exist in that same invisible space that the wireless internet, radio waves and GPS signals live. Some call it Heaven, I call it the Hereafter. We are literally 'here,' just 'after' and invisible, yet our energy still exists.

We human beings have three main fears: the fear of dying, the fear of failure and the fear of being alone. If people truly believed in life after death, do you think our lives might be different? To not fear death means not fearing life! Imagine yourself courageously going after a dream and achieving it? If we do not die, we cannot possibly fail. Life, I say, is an education for the soul. We learn from every experience, good and bad. Also, I believe that those we have loved and lost are not gone, including our pets. Keep talking to them. They can hear you and you will see them again. I'd bet my life on it.

Were you able to keep your mind open and not let any negative self-talk sneak in while reading this? It takes practice, lots of it, and I don't think it ever gets easy. My goal was to start opening your mind and hopefully get you on track to shifting your beliefs. You, my friend, are a whole lot more incredible than the skin and bones that you are made of. This world is a magical place, trust me.

There is a whole lot more I'd like to share with you. I have some daily practices that will help 'supercharge' you and help you get some new results in your life much faster. If you are interested, I'd be happy to send them to you with a few other fun gifts. Please visit my webpage at
www.wedontdie.com/shiftyourbeliefs.html

About the Author

Sandra Champlain had a fear of dying that led her on a 15-year journey to find proof of life after death. Too afraid of being ridiculed, she remained quiet about her findings. After the death of her father, Sandra created "How to Survive Grief," a free audio that was quickly heard by thousands worldwide. Armed with this powerful information that has reduced pain and saved lives, she courageously wrote the now #1 international bestseller *We Don't Die - A Skeptic's Discovery of Life After Death*. Sandra is the subject of the video documentary "'We Don't Die," by Emmy Award-winning filmmaker, Robert Lyon, and her interview is featured in the book *Conversations with Visionary Entrepreneurs* with Tim Ferriss.

Sandra is a highly respected speaker, author and entrepreneur committed to making a difference in the lives of others. She lives in Byfield, Massachusetts.

To learn more or to contact Sandra, please visit www.wedontdie.com

Life From Here to There

Cindy Halley

One day, much to my surprise, I woke up in the *middle* of my life and asked myself, "How did I get here?" Have you ever asked yourself the same question?

I knew what I was doing each day, but I wasn't aware of *how* I lived my life and *how* that affected me — and everyone else. I remember clearly looking around as if to find the answer written down somewhere. I told myself that I was a "smart girl," but, somehow, everything was messed up. And I was clueless. This is not the life I planned. Life always moved quickly for me, and I liked it like that. The quickness and speed with which I lived my life was exciting and spontaneous, yet never allowed me to evaluate how I was doing. My goal was to keep moving on to bigger and better things. And if that didn't work, well, I would always find another better plan, *not really* taking the time to sit and think about any consequences. If I made bad decisions, what the hell. Tomorrow would be a better day. If I lost a job, I could always get a new one. Tomorrow would be better day. Anyone would be lucky to have me. I worked hard and I played hard; I was a survivor. Heck! If you knew what I had to go through, you probably would have given me a medal! And that is truly what I thought. The life I was living was for having fun — and who wouldn't want that?

I thought I deserved to have the attitude of "this is *my* time." I could do whatever and whomever I wanted. I was slim, attractive, educated and fun! But when the party was over, and the people were gone, I was left with a feeling of lack. In fact, *if* I thought about it, I was sad. If I *really* looked at myself, I would cry, because I felt alone, isolated and unloved. I needed more fun and more people around. Who wants to be around someone who has depressed thoughts or feelings? I wasn't aware that I was living a double life: one that I would show other people, and the other for when I was alone. This worked for a long time...but on that day, the day when I woke up, it stopped working.

What stopped working was the "numbing effect" of drinking and partying. Having a couple of drinks or smoking a little pot kept me mellow, because I was high energy — and that was the story I told myself. In fact, I believed most of the stories I told myself. And if one didn't work, I would make up another story. That pattern lasted a long time. So I was constantly telling myself stories about me and my life. I had to believe them, because if I didn't believe them, how were the people around me going to believe them? They may even see through me and see the real me, and I couldn't afford that. Inevitably, some people did see me and what was happening, and that scared me! I knew that when they actually saw the "bullshit," I would get "the look." Have you ever seen the look? It's the nonverbal message expressing disdain, disappointment and disapproval. That brought up the worst feelings. It felt like I was turned inside out, plummeting in a downward spiral into my acidic, aching stomach.

Conversations That Make a Difference

And then in one instant — composure. I found myself once again saying, "It's not that bad; tomorrow will be better. I promise!" But I knew deep down that I couldn't keep that promise. It wasn't going to be better. It would be even worse if I didn't numb myself again. That was the secret I kept. I knew I couldn't stop. I didn't stop earlier because of the pain from my past. Now I couldn't stop because the drinking and drugs took hold of me. I now *needed* to drink — but I didn't *want* to drink.

This is what is called the "jumping off place." You can't go back and it's hard to go forward. I know *now* that there is no problem in the world that doesn't have a Spiritual Solution, but at first that didn't sit right with me. I was raised Catholic, and that sounded religious! That "God thing" worked for others, but God left me a long time ago. Yet I took the leap anyway! I had no problem leaping. Hey, in my past, I was always leaping from one thing to another. But I knew I didn't have a grasp on this one. By the grace of God, I found the solution to help me look at things a little differently. I was willing, but I was also afraid.

I didn't realize what a fearful, unaware life I was living until I actually looked at myself. I was fearful of the pain of the past that always haunted me, so I drank to silence the memories. Before I could even look back, I had to lay a good foundation for myself.

"Addiction is any container that holds your spirit. It could be alcohol, drugs, shopping, sex, Facebook, reading, television – anything that keeps you separated from your spirit and living the life of your dreams." ~ Roi Solberg

I was willing to admit that drinking was just a symptom of my problems. I knew my life was a little messy, but I never thought it was unmanageable, or that I had insane thinking! In time, I came to realize that the "story" of "it's not so bad" was coming from my ego. My ego had to be smashed. I was doing the same thing over and over again and expecting different results — and that is INSANE. So I surrendered my old way of thinking and learned "acceptance" — with a new perspective. This was the key, to learn to look at life and myself, to see exactly what is for the way it is. And not the way I wanted it to be or how I thought it should be. I acknowledged that I had a physical allergy, mental immaturity and was spiritually bankrupt. I knew in my heart of hearts that I couldn't do this alone. But I didn't know where or how to start!

It was suggested that I get on my knees and ask "the God of my understanding" to remove the obsession. I resisted that...but one day I was struggling so badly with the obsession to drink that, in the middle of the afternoon, in the middle of my living room, I broke down, as desperate as can be! I remember in that pivotal moment saying, *"God, take this from me."* Time stood still. I really can't remember how much time passed, but to my surprise, I felt relief! I really felt it! And at that moment, I "owned" the experience that God touched me and was listening. This truly was one of my Spiritual Transformations!

Every time I surrender, a door opens and I know God is listening. I know I have to listen as well. Since developing a relationship with GOD, I now take time in the morning to get on my knees and ask God to direct me during the day. And every time I ASK, I find my day runs more smoothly.

That experience gave me the hope and courage to continue on my journey. My journey had to start in the past — not in the future of tomorrows. And there, I found my "childhood victim" — and victims don't recover! I discovered that you can rewrite your past. I went back as an adult with new eyes and looked at my life, like the ghost of Christmas past. I saw a lonely little girl who thought she was abandoned, unloved and alone, living in a hopeless environment. I now had the wonderful opportunity to save her! I embraced her and revealed a clear and detailed account of the surrounding circumstances. Today as a loving reminder, I carry a picture of myself as a 3-year-old. I now know that life isn't perfect, that people aren't perfect, and that I had a "supporting role" to impact those imperfect people — and I learned forgiveness and the ability to let go of any hope of a better past.

GOD was with me all along. He gave me the gift of perseverance, emotional honesty and a pursuit of independent thinking — and most of all, the gift of comedic relief. I was, and am, a child of GOD. I just forgot. I do not want to shut the door to those experiences, because they have created the person I am today. I have a new freedom, a new happiness and a strong determination to be the best version of myself, with the help of a loving GOD. I do my best, I show up and I serve with gratitude. I may not know what the next right thing is, but I know I can do the next thing right. I do my best. My best is different on different days, and that is okay! It is spiritual progress, rather than spiritual perfection. I do not strive for perfection, because that is unattainable, but I keep striving! And when old character defects pop up, I recognize them for what they are — old fears manifesting with different faces.

Today, I can pause, be still and experience the healing possibilities that come from prayer and meditation. As a result, I get the answers that I already knew I had within. More will be revealed when I am ready, when all is aligned just the way it should be! I now realize that acceptance is the key to all my unanswered questions. But the best part is at the end of my day. I get on my knees and say, "Thank you," for life is bountiful. I am ever reminding myself, "I am an instrument of GOD, with infinite love and joy."

And as I continue on my journey, I realize that my mission all along has been to share with others the gifts that I've received. Do you believe that you *have* the answers available to you? Are you willing to be open and honest with yourself? So here we are. Inspired and knowing that great things will happen. Are you ready?

In the Spirit of the Light,

A person just like you.

P.S. Non-believers welcomed!

About the Author

Cindy Halley
aka "The GODpillow Lady", in her entertaining style, speaks at workshops and expos around the country, sharing her story of recovery. Created during her own recovery, Cindy's GODpillow products, now embroidered in four different languages, are inspirational reminders designed to help you create a balance of body, mind and spirit as you focus on healing. Since 2003, the "GODpillow Family" has grown to more than 5,000 members in 10 countries. Visit www.godpillow.com.

Follow Cindy on Facebook:
www.facebook.com/cindy.rosenthalhalley,
Join the GODpillow Community:
www.facebook.com/GODpillowLady

Cindy is also a Certified LifeLine practitioner. The LifeLine technique is a holistic system designed by Dr. Darren Weissman, to uncover, release and interpret the root cause of physical symptoms and stress. Having experienced transformation in just one session, Cindy became a believer, a practitioner and now a promoter of Dr. Darren's mission of *"world peace is through inner peace."*

Check out www.open2thejourney.com or follow www.facebook.com/Open2theJourney

Shift Your Beliefs to Get What You Want

Wake Up to the Universal God

Steven E. Schmitt

Before moving further I would like to explain what I mean by the universal God-force within you. When you go back in history and look at the great teachers of religions and doctrines such as Christianity, Buddhism, Judaism, Islam, Sufism, and Confucianism, they have all left us with the same message; God is within us, God is love, the Holy Spirit is inside you, the Father and I are one.

I think the book *A Course In Miracles* said it the best:

> *"The only problem we have is when we think we are separate from the God that is within us."*

We hear this same message everywhere in the world by Jesus Christ, Buddha and all of the other supreme spiritual beings that have lived on our planet. All have similar messages about the universal God-force being within us and outside of us. But, what exactly are they pointing to?

The truth is that, try as we may, no one will ever be able to fully prove its existence, but if we take a serious look at the subtle forces guiding the process of growth, then we can get a glimpse into how this energy guides our life. First and foremost, this energy is in everything; in every atom that makes up our whole universe. The universal God-force is eternally good, joyous, loving and infinitely abundant. Think of how your hair or fingernails grow, or how your skin regenerates itself. This process uses the same energy that makes plants and trees grow. If we are going to have any sort of role model that we aspire to, we should liken ourselves to this universal God-force.

I have found that the only way you can really get to know the universal God-force is through meditation or chanting. The reason why is that when you meditate or chant, you transcend the mind. Knowing God just by intellect is like knowing how to lose weight or eat healthy food; you know how to lose weight but you do not do it by experience. It is only lip service. Once you learn how to meditate or chant, then you can be the universal God-force, and you will see this energy in everyone and in all things. You will not just know about God by reading spiritual books, you will have God in your life at all times. We are all a part of the universal God-force. Like I said, we must learn to transcend the mind and this is why you need to learn to meditate.

Meditation is like plugging into God's electrical circuit board — you become instantly energized. You become more peaceful and more aware of creation. It releases stress and creates a doorway to your true self. You can dissolve your doubts, negativity, and fears through being and knowing that you are part of the universal God-force. You nourish your soul through meditation.

Meditation is like reading any spiritual or holy book only one million times more potent. When you do your own work to connect to this energy, the universe is opened to you as a co-creator.

There are also many medical benefits associated with meditation. Your internal soul-force is stimulated; you enjoy deep relaxation as blood pressure and heart rate regulate, thereby reducing the workload on the heart.

If God is only love, good and is infinite abundance and you are part of God, what if you shift your thoughts as God thoughts? Your actions would produce a very rich and happy life. Really, the only problem we ever have is when we are not connected to the God that is part of us.

About the Author

Steven E. Schmitt is a family man who has over 30 bestselling books known in the U.S. and internationally. His work has sold more books than 99% of the authors on the planet. Do you have a favorite inspirational author or speaker? It is likely that Steven has worked with them.

Steven speaks to thousands of people on how to find their life purpose and develop a passion for what they do. He has spent his adult life as an entrepreneur building financially successful businesses. Steven is an inspirational speaker helping people awaken to their potential on a physical, emotional and spiritual level.

Steven is the founder of the Wake Up Spiritual Center.

His websites:

WakeUpSpiritualCenter.com

BestSellerGuru.com

Shift Your Beliefs to Get What You Want

I Have a Gift For You!

Lee Beard

Go with me on an odyssey to find what could be the greatest gift of your life. When I checked the definition of "odyssey", it described our life journey. Odyssey: a long wandering or voyage usually marked by many changes of fortune; an intellectual or spiritual wandering or quest.

As we venture together, look for the treasure or the gift that relates to your current experience. My quest for several years has been to discover a foundation for my business and my life. I had a great home life growing up and I was given a faith foundation that my parents lived every day and with more of my own study, has come more practical revelation.

My experiences in the entertainment, sports, marketing and publishing world has given me a broad background in business. For the last few years, I have been developing a business structure for my family which has evolved into working with business owners as well as their families. The family of the owners and the families of the staff that work in the company are *all* affected by the success of the business.

Many years ago, I was told that most people are searching for security in their business and their life. This brought me to creating a program for business owners, their families and their staff to prepare for successful transition of the ownership of the business called *Secure Transition*. I realized that the ownership of the business will be transitioned for one of many reasons; but will it be a secure transition?

Security requires a solid, unshakeable foundation. So how can that be accomplished? What is unshakable and lasting to the end? What is it that is part of both business and personal relationships that creates that unshakeable foundation?

It seems that love is universal and essential to all of our lives. So to have love in your life as a core foundation would be a good place to start. This is reinforced by the scripture 1 Corinthians 13:13 *But now faith, hope, love, abide these three; but the greatest of these is love.*

So what is love?

Love is patient, love is kind and is not jealous; love does not brag and is not arrogant, does not act unbecomingly; it does not seek its own, is not provoked, does not take into account a wrong suffered, does not rejoice in unrighteousness, but rejoices with the truth; bears all things, believes all things, hopes all things, endures all things. Love never fails;
~ *from 1 Corinthians 13:4-8a*

Who, or what, is our best example of love? In the scriptures, 1 John 4:16 tell us: *God is love*. So, if God is love, I took the liberty to replace the word love from the scripture above and inserted God as follows:

God is patient, God is kind and is not jealous; God does not brag and is not arrogant, does not act unbecomingly;

God does not seek His own, is not provoked, does not take into account a wrong suffered, does not rejoice in unrighteousness, but rejoices with the truth; bears all things, believes all things, hopes all things, endures all things. God never fails.

How does God express His love? He is a gift giver. This is evidenced through scripture in John 3:16: *God so loved the world that He gave His only Son.* Jesus also tells us in John 15:10: *Just as the Father has loved Me, I have also loved you; abide in My love.*

This gift of love is for you to the end! As you explore farther, you will discover more about how God loves you and the security that He brings to your life.

The gift of this day, today, is a great example of His love. Enjoy the gift of His love for you today!

All scriptures are taken from the context section at http://biblehub.com

About the Author

Lee Beard is the creator of the Secure Transition program which is a unique approach to security and sustainability from the teachings of Jesus. Working through relationships and referrals, he prepares practical, custom strategies for entrepreneurs and business leaders fashioned after his current businesses. Knowing the ownership of all businesses will change, the most important question is "are you in control now and will you be in control to the end of the process?" If your answer to this question is maybe, we need to talk. Drawing from many years of business and family experience, Lee Beard has developed a proven multifaceted, specialist team method to assist with building a secure legacy.

To learn more, go to:
http://securetransition.com and
http://leebeard.net/

Happiness is a Choice...It is YOURS to Make

Lorane Gordon

Childhood guilt is a choking sensation; a lump being pushed down your throat till it sits in your stomach, heavy, like a rock, weighing you down. The sound of the glass shower door shattering on my sister and I when we were 6 and 8 was simply terrifying, bewildering and in some way, my fault. I could not, at that time, understand the pain my mother was in as she kicked in the glass in another one of her crazy mood swings; children just accept the blame.

My escape was lying on the grass, visualizing the clouds enveloping me in their soft puffiness, carrying me away from the fear and insecurity. The clouds formed dreams, imagined places in which I saw myself and my future. They were marshmallow chariots offering solace and glimpses of freedom. To this day, clouds are still a peaceful place in my world.

Understanding that there is another way, an answer out there in the universe is a complex concept for a child but at the same time, naturally inviting. Universal consciousness is the concept that the thoughts of all, from the infant to the aged, from the brilliant to the ordinary, are combined into a collective intelligence that you can tune into. By accessing that intelligence, somehow questions can be answered, control can be achieved and safety and security would be the outcome. This was an early, naïve but instinctive connection to the power of manifestation; the start of a journey that would challenge and eventually reveal a lot of truths.

Books, powerful books, were my salvation. *The Power of Positive Thinking*, by Norman Vincent Peale, was read with a passion at age thirteen. Thinking in a certain way and projecting those thoughts was the promise of everything I was looking for. I was manifesting into my personal reality a better way, a better life.

"Formulate and stamp indelibly on your mind a mental picture of yourself as succeeding," Peale wrote. *"Hold this picture tenaciously. Never permit it to fade. Your mind will seek to develop the picture.... Do not build up obstacles in your imagination."*

The rock of guilt had travelled to my heart causing self-doubt, depression, despair; the desperate search for happiness had begun and the *Power of Positive Thinking* offered hope, and a way out, a path to a more harmonious way of being. The adolescent me manifested her favorite meals, avoiding the dreaded broccoli! Boyfriends, good grades at school; anything that could be imagined was imagined and so began a fascination for the power of the mind. What was forming at that time would become not only my passion but my life's work.

Imagine sitting at the feet of masters whose whole lives have been focused on spiritual connection. The universe conspired in a way that allowed me to meet and observe those powerful people who used the very skills that fascinated me so much. Learning from the master hypnotist who used the technique of regression, to take a woman back to a lifetime she experienced in the 1600s. Listening to her speak clearly in a Slavic language that she had no knowledge of in the present day opened my mind to alternate realities. To me, that was proof there was much more to our existence than we could even imagine — and certainly more than I had been taught.

The journey to understanding was not without mistakes. The decision to leave a foolish marriage was followed by some hard partying and a wasteful time of indiscretion with the wrong people. I was behaving as an adult child with no plan for life and not caring about the consequences of my actions which eventually left me feeling empty. This is not unusual; we all sometimes stop and say to ourselves, "Is this all there is to life?" How many of us then decide to do something about it?

The relationship most of us want includes a feeling of security, stability a life of love with the "right one." I decided I needed to find that sort of relationship. Throughout the years I worked with different spiritual study groups on my ability to send messages. I became proficient at transmitting my thoughts to others in the group. The ability to receive messages and thoughts was less strong; this would be something needed in later life and would become part of my true awakening.

When you set your mind to it, you can make powerful events occur. Creating the life you want is a combination of desire and focus. Daydreaming, visualizing, writing down every detail in the present tense were the methods that had worked before and now worked again. I was seeing the man of my dreams in specific detail; walking up to the door of my beautiful home in my minds' eye, over and over again.

Conversations That Make a Difference

Projecting those thoughts into the universe with absolute conviction that this was my life was my tool for manifesting what I desired. The result? Six months later I was married to a wonderful man and living in a beautiful home, all as seen in my imagination.

That was thirty-three years ago.

I have always walked and talked my passion. Everyone around me, willing or not, became my student. Soon, it became my vocation and I was coaching an eager few. They were learning and doing quite well in their manifestations, and everything was terrific. Until it wasn't.

Remember how effective I was at sending, but not so good at receiving? Visualization and manifestation are great when you are lying on the grass looking at clouds; or listening to beautiful calming music, or lying in your expensive hot tub in your expensive house with an enviable lifestyle...until the universe sends you a rude awakening!

One day, while floating in the huge hot tub, in the beautiful backyard of my grand home, busily visualizing having even more wealth and material things; I was stunned when I clearly heard the words, *"So what?"* Shocked out of my reverie, I jumped up because it was as if the words were coming from someone standing above me. No one was there. I decided I must have imagined it, so I slid back into the warm water to continue visualizing greater things — more money, more this, more that — and I heard it again! What the hell did it mean? I was bewildered but ignored the voice.

This event marked the beginning of another stage in my life. I continued ignoring that "So what" voice and became very sick, spending the better part of a year in bed. My inability to respond to this warning message from the universe was literally, physically, ruining my life.

Shift Your Beliefs to Get What You Want

What is important to understand is that the universe is not cruel; it tries to teach you to connect with what is relevant, significant and what truly matters. It will send help when you need it, as long as you can recognize the message and the help. Help arrived for me in the shape of a good friend. My dear friend, knowing that I was in a bad place, sick at heart and in body arranged a trip to India. She insisted that I go with her.

The trip to India was an opportunity to take part in a retreat led by Dr. Deepak Chopra, a teacher I deeply respect. On the way to the airport, I picked up a book, *The Power of Now*, Eckhart Tolle's seminal work on living in the present moment. The concepts in that book seemed simple, yet layered in unexpected ways. During the flight, I read each chapter and then carefully summarized and explained the meaning of what I had read to my friend and traveling companion. Doing so allowed me to better understand the book, and step by step I began to internalize its power into my being. That book was manna for my starved soul. Though I didn't realize it at the time, living in the present moment would become my salvation, and it would be another way of living that I would teach to others.

The universe had literally spoken to me...it just took me over a year to listen! Having finally listened, the realization was that my belief system had revolved around projecting, sending, asking and insisting that what I wanted would appear in my reality. My beliefs shifted toward understanding the true spirituality of giving as well as receiving, of understanding the universe had an even better plan and that happiness came in more forms than material things.

Surprisingly, it hardly mattered that I went to India to learn from one of the best New Thought teachers in the world in an atmosphere of serene beauty. My whole purpose in taking that journey was to learn how living in the present moment allowed me to be happy. Happiness no longer depended on anything other than accepting the present moment. The discovery that happiness is a choice and by choosing happiness, one's conscious manifestations became easy and a natural occurrence formed my teachings from then on. Most importantly, I found that maintaining the power of happiness created an energy field that attracts positive things, making both conscious and unconscious manifestation so much easier and even more rewarding. Finally, I had discovered my mantra, happiness first...the rest will follow.

Returning home from India, my natural path was to once again put out my shingle as a teacher and a coach. Soon, many people were coming to me and lives were being changed. Other than the birth of my son, nothing in the world gave me as much pleasure as seeing my own students going from unhappy to happy, from despair to hopefulness. This was my nourishment. This was my reason for being — and it still is.

My journey has allowed me to incorporate all of my knowledge into programs that promote happiness. I now realize that I strove for material things in the past to make myself happy, and I now understand that I could never enjoy the very things I manifested because my mindset was all about getting more and more things.

Combining my manifestation skills with living in the present moment allows me to have all the things I want in my life — and, most importantly, enjoy life in this moment...and this moment...and this moment. This is how I can have my cake and eat it, too. I teach and coach my Happiness programs all over the world via webinars on the Internet and over Skype. I know that my reason for being is to teach, and everything I have learned is to be passed on to others for the greater good of all.

Past struggles are lessons we learn from. Once you have learned the lesson the struggle is teaching you; those types of situations no longer appear in your life. Living in the present moment and understanding you have the choice to be happy shifts your focus away from seeing the negative, toward seeing the positive. This awareness tunes you in to the messages from your higher self which will happily keep you on your soul's path. CHOOSE happiness first...and the rest will follow.

About the Author

Lorane Gordon is an inspirationalist, a major manifester herself and an expert in the fields of Law of Attraction and Present Moment Awareness is once again bringing her dynamic, loving and inspirational teachings to the world. After a ten-year period of perfecting her message she has burst forth on the scene stronger than ever. Lorane gives you the tools to manifest the life of your dreams and a life of happiness. She lives by her mantra, *happiness first...the rest will follow* and wants others to be able to do the same!

Lorane is loved by her students and teachers alike, in fact Deepak Chopra was moved to write *"Lorane Gordon is a teacher of infinite possibilities."*

Lorane's intent is to bring happiness into as many lives as possible which is the driving force behind her new set of programs, "*Happiness First... the rest will follow.*"

http://HappinessFirstBook.com
www.LoraneGordon.com
lorane@LoraneGordon.com
www.facebook.com/yourhappinessway
www.twitter.com/loranegordon
www.pinterest.com/loranegordon/

I Found Happiness by Learning the Truth and Shedding the Lies

Joe Dichiara

I was alone, miserable, financially and emotionally bankrupt and worse of all, I had no idea why!

What drives us? What makes us do the things we do? I'm not talking about motivation. We can get motivated but what drives us is something a lot deeper. We can consciously set goals, have ambitions and expectations but don't always get to the place we had planned on, while others seem to achieve the impossible. It turns out that what is really driving us are our beliefs. Our core beliefs are working in the background telling us that we can do this or we can't do that. What if what we believe is not always the truth? Not a lie but a misconception based on what we were taught, growing up. This is what I have come to understand as a "false belief." We believe almost everything we are taught by the people closest to us; our family, teachers, friends. Most of them are people we don't get to choose.

We download a tremendous amount of information, learned responses, fears, impressions, expectations and more throughout our lives. This information and our experiences shape our beliefs to the very core of our souls and make us into the men and women we are today. These beliefs are what ultimately drive us to do the things we do, to make the decisions we make; whether we realize it or not. We act in certain ways through our subconscious mind while we believe we are making conscious decisions. I hate to tell you this folks, but the truth is that most of us do things and never even know why. This is where my quest for over-analyzing everything has taken me.

To be honest, it's all pretty complicated to me. Conscious, subconscious, false beliefs, etc... All I know is that I came to a point in my life when too many of these so-called "false beliefs" came crashing down on me, seemingly all at once. I was alone, miserable, financially and emotionally bankrupt and, worst of all, I had no idea why. I knew hundreds of people, had plenty of clients that needed me and a big family that loved me; yet I felt trapped, isolated and all alone. All I knew was that there was a time in my life I thought I had everything I needed to be happy - a wife, kids, successful business, house, nice car. I was living the proverbial American dream. Things were looking good and the future looked even better. I wondered how my life shifted from that "comfortable/happy" place to a deep, dark cold place. It was the exact opposite of what I had planned.

There were two things that were certain to me:

1. I was in a miserable place.
2. Something had to change or I would be trapped there forever.

The only question became, "What exactly had to change?" At least I knew change was possible. If it wasn't, why would I even bother? Next, if it was possible, how was it possible? In other words - give me the damn instructions! This is one of the issues I have always had with a pre-determined destiny. If God already has my plan worked out then I must just be an observer, right? Confusion. Read the Bible, more confusion. Read *Think and Grow Rich*, more confusion. Try Yoga, more confusion. Therapy, more confusion. Medication, twelve step programs.....I didn't understand anything except that the more information and practice I engaged in, the more pain, misery and confusion I experienced.

In April of 2009, in my continuous search for answers to questions I wasn't really sure of, I read yet another book, this one was called, *The Science of Getting Rich* by Wallace Wattles. I was drawn to it because of a movie called *The Secret* by Rhonda Byrne. The movie was based on the ideas she read in the book, *The Science of Getting Rich*. The movie, at the time, became pretty popular and was featured on Oprah Winfrey's television show, *Oprah*. It all had to do with "manifesting" things into your life. The concept was to think of it something hard enough, long enough and with enough belief, and you can make it happen. In other words - visualize it, believe it and achieve it. It seemed pretty obscure to me, but finally something started to make sense. Some of it seemed to be repeating the same information I had already "downloaded." At a desperate point in her life, Rhonda Byrne's daughter handed her a book and said, "This might help." The book was *The Science of Getting Rich*.

The book was an easy read, only about 96 pages and the theory seemed pretty simple, almost too simple. Mr. Wattles writes that there is an exact science to getting "rich" and it works the same as any other universal law. The same way that $1 + 1 = 2$. It doesn't matter what your past or present circumstances are, it will work 100% of the time. All you have to do is "Start thinking a certain way." I was convinced that this guy really believed what he was writing and most of it seemed connected to a lot of what I had read and felt about success and happiness. Mr. Wattles' conviction was summed up in his challenge that *"if just one person follows the exact instructions in this book and does not get rich, it is proof that his theory is false. But if everyone that follows the instructions gets rich, that is proof that his science is correct."*

I decided to take him up on the challenge. There was no downside. All I had to do was *"start thinking in a certain way."* This is where the real journey began for me. Up until this point in my life, I really didn't know what the point of my life was. It was obvious that the way I thought I had been thinking up to this point was exactly what got me where I was. Was it possible that my thinking had gotten twisted? Why hadn't I gotten the results I had expected? I think it just came down to the fact that I thought that all I had to do was make a lot of money to be successful.

Let me be clear here: I was not living a completely miserable life. Most of my life was fantastic, happy and abundant. I have had personal, family and financial success. The issue for me was that it wasn't the kind of success that last forever. Most of it seemed fleeting.

With the new knowledge I had, I realized a rich, fulfilling life was possible and Wallace Wattles had given me the exact instructions. With an open mind I began reading and listening to The Science of Getting Rich. Over and over again, I took in the words and concepts until they became etched in my mind. I began thinking about changing my view on business. I start "THINKING" in a creative way instead of a competitive way. One of the instructions I worked with is to be for people instead of against people. Additionally, most of the things I was learning from the book were things I already believed. I believed these things but didn't understand how to apply them to my life and business; they are also keys to being successful and happy at the same time.

As I think about that, I realize that I had to define what it meant to be happy and successful in both business and in my personal life. That's what I really wanted. Happy and successful to me means loving what I do all the time, whether it's helping someone, making money or spending time with my family and friends. What Mr. Wattles was offering me was the opportunity to have all of this at the same time, plus he claimed that we were entitled to it and it was our God given duty to claim it; not only for ourselves, for the whole world! Our success has a ripple effect and God created us to be prosperous. He supplied unlimited abundance and it is all there for us as long as we "think" in a certain way.

This is how it works - people who are intelligent, talented and beautiful don't automatically get "rich." In fact, many of them never get rich and people who are broke become rich, people who are not smart and/or beautiful become rich. Also people from one place get rich while people in the same place don't get rich. People with the same education, connections and resources get rich while other don't get rich. People that are born into wealth lose it while people that are born broke get rich. People of a certain religion get rich while people of the same religion never get rich. The point is that it does not matter what your circumstances are, everyone can become rich.

Thinking a certain way has to lead to acting a certain way, which can only really happen when you start believing a certain way. As it turns out, thinking a certain way was all about Faith in God. If the author had immediately revealed this, I probably would not have been as drawn to it as I was. It was all so simple and perfect. The proof was everywhere. It can be seen in history and in the world around us. What seemed complicated in the past was laid out in front of me in black and white. We co-create with God based on thinking a certain way. If I have faith in God and believe He can do anything then actually, I should be able to do anything. Knowing it and doing it are two totally different things.

Little by little, one onion skin at a time, I started shedding my old, false beliefs. I'm still shedding them today, learning new things about myself and the world. Replacing old, false beliefs with the truth and gaining new experiences, with a whole new perspective. I have something today that is priceless; I am at peace and completely comfortable with who I am, what I'm responsible for and more important, what I am capable of with God by my side. I have actually been able to relinquish the job of running the universe and saving the world! Imagine that! It was nice to find out that this was His job all along and the only job I have is to be the best, most prosperous person I can be.

Today, life is good! It's as simple as that. I am living, growing, learning and experiencing. I have never, ever been happier and the truth is, when I look at it - I have all of the same "stuff" that I had all along. Of course, I still have some of the same life stuff that we all have, like paying bills, health, family and the day to day happening of everyday life. In the same way I still have a good business, a great family, tons of friends. The truth is I have always had everything I ever needed to be successful and happy. It was always there for the taking and was given freely to me. I was blind and deaf to it. A relationship with Him is all I ever needed yet, I didn't know how or why. I was given a new perspective and it has made all the difference.

Looking back, I thought my shift started the day I picked up that book, but it was actually a process that was started long ago. The real truth is this: I had to go through all of the pain and suffering I went through so I could start thinking His way instead of my way. God was always there just waiting for me to decide. I don't think my beliefs actually shifted, It was my understanding of them that made all the difference for me. I was taught all the right things as I was growing up but my own misperceptions created those dreadful "false beliefs." There is peace and serenity when you know the Truth!

About the Author

Joe DiChiara has a passion for helping individuals succeed in business and believes that the American dream is still alive and well. An accomplished CPA and Entrepreneur, Mr. DiChiara has worked with thousands of small businesses while successfully starting, buying and selling several of his own businesses.

He opened his first CPA office in 1994 specializing in solving tax problems. By 1996 he had expanded his business by providing QuickBooks training and support to small businesses. In 2004 he developed an online bookkeeping system that substantially reduces admin costs for business. Today he teaches his Bookkeeping Success System to individuals who have no prior bookkeeping skills. Several have had great success in their own businesses as a result.

You can learn more about Mr. DiChiara and his Entrepreneur and Bookkeeping Success Systems by visiting www.joedichiara.biz

Failing Forward Fast for Financial Freedom

Patricia Giankas

Can you say *challenges?* After both my daughter and step daughter were diagnosed with thyroid cancer, my husband got diagnosed with arrhythmias. My son, Adrian, had surgery to fix a broken nose. Jim, my step son, had a double hernia operation. Vanessa, my daughter, and Toula, Jim's wife, had a major car accident. Karen and Vanessa, my two daughters, were involved in a car accident in which Karen's pelvic bone was dislodged. She was pregnant at that time. All of this happened within a period of 6 months during 2007. During the following year, Karen gave birth to my beautiful grandson, Matthew, who was ill for almost the first full year of his life.

A group of people wanted to partner with me in business, but had ulterior motives to take my company from me. This caused me to lose control of my business. That event and all of the unexpected family happenings was like a house of cards falling for a period of a year right in front of me. I could not stop it and I could not catch up with it.

The following year, I merged my business with another company. In that process, I discovered that, as much as I know about business, not all is what it seems. People can say want they want, but don't necessarily follow through and unfortunately, whether intended or not, wreak havoc on lots of lives. Challenges indeed!

In an effort to maintain the office and the business, I cashed in my life savings and sold all my properties. I was not ready to walk away from the business and the building that was my life. Gratefully, family and friends stepped in to help me financially in an effort to keep the business from crumbling. Emotionally and physically I suffered through a period of transition with sleepless nights and pure exhaustion. I began asking God, "Why and how did this happen to me?"

Prior to asking that question, I was living in survival mode, doing everything I could to keep the business together just to make ends meet. Unconsciously, I didn't realize that even without any money to speak of, God was providing for us. We never went without a meal or bills being paid. There were still past clients and referrals who were enough, just enough, to get us through.

After feeling completely rejected, I even felt as if my home that I had lived in for eighteen years was rejecting me. Finally, after much despair and deliberation, I made a decision to sell that home and move into a rental. A burden was lifted. My office building lease had come due at the same time. Ten thousand square feet of office furniture and my house got moved in the same day.

A New Beginning
Out of that darkness emerged light and the hope for the future.

I needed something. All the dreams I was having while I slept were dark and so many people were depending on me.

What to do? I finally began to seek spiritual help and guidance. I had been having vivid dreams that I was running in and from a dark place. If there is such a thing as hell, I felt as if I was there. I consulted Sophia Rouchotas of Eagle Den Healing. She helped me out of the darkness I was living in by clearing my energy, counseling me and holding my hand through the sale of the house I had bought in 1978; my first house. We went to the house together and I thought I felt her helping me shovel a path in waist high snow, through the wide driveway to the house. I looked back once I reached the front door and Sophia was still standing at the bottom of the driveway. I asked her how she got there so fast. She said she'd never moved. I *know* I had help!

Somehow, I knew that the single picture of an owl I found in the laundry room that day, at least according to Sophia's belief, was a good sign. As we left, Sophia noticed that each of the windows of the house next door to my house had an owl in the windows. I listed the house and sold it 3 days later for the asking price. I began to feel better as I realized there needed to be a time to appreciate the light that would come from the darkness. When I was a child, my father and I would go with him to the villages to preach the sermon, he was a priest. I remember a prayer that says even Jesus descended into Hell before He rose to heaven. By releasing that house, I was letting go of the past and the horror show that was my life. I was open to the light and goodness to come.

Once I opened up to spiritual growth, I was introduced to many people in the healing and helping fields; it was the law of attraction bringing them into my life. I began giving my support to others in any way I could, including financially, even though, at that time, I didn't have money to give. It just always seemed to show up at the right time. No matter what

Conversations That Make a Difference

I needed, it was provided for me. It was time to get humble and since then, God has never stopped providing for me.

When you have had it all, then have nothing, something needs to shift. I was riding the wave of wealth without feeling the gratitude for what I had. My dreams have always kept me in check. When everything was tumbling and crumbling around me, I dreamed of myself in a hole, unable to get out. Now I dream of walking on water with Jesus, climbing mountains, with Him *always* reaching to help me.

In 2010, I moved into a rental property that was a gift from God. It was listed for sale or rent and the last house we were going to look at, completely out of our area. My daughter and I fell in love with the home; it was perfect for us. It was a stepping stone to where we are now. It gave me time to follow through on my intention to pay back those who helped me restart my life.

Clients were showing up, people were calling. Since 2009, I have been riding the wave of God's grace. The flood gates of heavenly blessings have opened and have been blessing me, my family and my business since then.

Back in 2000 I gave a presentation to a group of people and a young lady named Anne Brill was there doing clerical work. I told her that she needed to become a mortgage broker. I didn't know that she would take my advice and go on to become a very successful broker. Then in August 2012, upon discovering three of my clients had previously mortgaged with Ann, I decided to call her and set a meeting. She reminded me of the advice I gave her, leading to her success. She credited me with her success. Ultimately, I invited her to become a partner in my business. Ann says, "In order to make the relationships in my life work, my biggest need is communication. I must have complete understanding with my husband and daughter as well as my business partner and colleagues. That's what makes this partnership one made in heaven."

At the same time, the software I had been building since 2005 became a merger of three different software programs I would use in my business. In May of 2012, I was introduced to Rusty Bresse. We contracted in August for the use of the software that I had envisioned and he had already developed. Years of work were saved, and another partnership from heaven was born. I flew, with my team, to his office in Milledgeville Ga., and within an hour, we realized that there had been a lifelong connection between us. Only spirit can put people together for the greatest good. We have since converted the software to Canadian as well. Rusty shares the same family values as me. He treats his staff with respect. He's adopted his step kids as his own and takes care of his ailing mother. I have gone to his home, stayed with his family, celebrated Shabbat on Friday and gone to Synagogue on Saturday. He welcomed me in as a family member. I've even met the most inspiring Rabbi through Rusty.

Both of my businesses have had new life breathed into them since 2012. What are the odds of these things falling into place? Many times we can take a message of hope out of our deepest darkest moments. If we can stay out of the question of "Why me?" we can find the answer without even asking the question. A different perspective or a shift in belief will have us changing our focus from what is keeping us in the darkness, to seeing the light which will lead us out.

Sometimes, in looking back we find just how far we have failed forward:

Conversations That Make a Difference

When I knew that my marriage had failed and I was trying to make it work back in 1990, I literally tore my house down and rebuilt a "monster home." We only lived in that house for two months after friends and family helped to complete it when the contractor disappeared with $200,000. Materials we had purchased to build the house were being put into other homes he contracted. I have actually lived to watch that contractor lose everything, having not done the right thing. He has since been divorced and lived in a basement apartment. Can you say Karma?? If I had only known then that I could shift my beliefs to get what I wanted, I would never have done business with him.

During that time, I also made the decision to leave my eighteen- year marriage. Instead of letting go of the marriage that I didn't realize was keeping me bound, I did all I could to make it work. There were so many signs and messages that came to me during that time, but I felt I had to do whatever it took to make it work. I didn't pay attention to the messages until I had an actual spiritual experience with Jesus himself in a ray of light in my bedroom where He told me not to worry, He would take care of everything for me. Today I am happily married for almost twenty-three years to Fred. He has been my pillar of strength for my children. He brought with him two wonderful children Kathren and Jim.

Even when we get advice and comfort from God Himself, we sometimes still think, for whatever reasons, things may work out if we stay in the place of darkness and despair. Maybe someone else will change and it will get better. Maybe I don't have to seek help from others to keep me safe. Maybe I don't have to use the 'built in courage' I came with. Even after that, I still did things on my own and messed up royally with the fall of my business, and the final breakup of my marriage. Life finally turned around when I recognized that I had to, once again, shift my belief.

As you climb the corporate ladder, people will try to pull you down. Watch for the telltale signs and keep shifting your belief to find the message in what is happening. With all the negativity surrounding these experiences, look for the positive hidden within. Something good comes out of everything. We may not know what it in that moment or during the happenings of the time, but it will always reveal itself.

In the last two years, I've looked back to 2001, which was the true beginning of my business life. Almost like a trip back in time, I've been climbing the ladder of success steadily with more knowledge, more experience, more awareness, more value of relationship, more spiritual centering. I feel as if all the connections I have been made over this time are ones that have always been. It's so comforting to know that I am embraced by the love and support of others and am able to be of support to others as well.

About the Author

Patricia Giankas brings over thirty years of experience in the Financial Services industry; leveraging her expertise and know-how. She realized the need for offering clients complete financial representation. She has been recognized in her field of expertise and has established a reputation as the true expert and leader in the mortgage industry.

Patricia's ability to connect with her dreams, has intrigued her and has kept her moving forward in her personal life and in business. Sharing her knowledge of wealth creation has brought her much personal satisfaction in that she has changed the lives of many.

Patricia has lectured at women shelters and the YWCA. She has provided assistance to community charities, bringing hope and help to various areas of the world. In this time where many people are turned upside down in their finance, Patricia helps them to make sense of their financial mess.

Connect with Patricia at p.giankas@score-up.ca

What's Your Ambition?

Doreen DeJesus

Having been recently divorced with two small children, I moved to New York in '93. While I was born in New York and had family there, it was not my home. Immediately upon arriving, I got offered a job in the financial industry. I had no training in the industry, but I was willing to learn and that was all that mattered. In order to fulfill the responsibilities of my new position I enrolled at NYU, and got my paralegal certificate. After only a year, I realized that my ambitions for myself had gone south. I needed something more, but I didn't know what, or how to get it while I was caught up in the day to day world of finance.

I was working as an office manager and paralegal. I was managing an administrative staff of eight people, and was one of two paralegals who the attorney I worked for had on staff. My typical day required me to handle all of the daily reporting for the department, manage the attorney's work and calendar, manage the administrative staff assigned to me, learn different software systems that were being utilized in the financial industry and train new administrative personnel as they came in.

Conversations That Make a Difference

I had a very unique position. It was very diverse, a combination of law and managerial. I was the first point of contact if there was an issue with a lawyer; I also had a typical office manager administrative role which also included hiring and firing the administrative staff that worked under my supervision. All this blended together for the overachiever personality that I have.

Managing an attorney in the mix was interesting. I made sure all of the documents were where they needed to be, the filings were all in the right courts, the discovery was complete and if the attorney was looking for a specific document, it was exactly where it needed to be. I managed the account, the trip schedules, made sure everything was booked for the trips, and ensured they had everything they needed. All of this happened at an extremely fast pace. Can you say *STRESS?*

Then, in 1997, I was involved in a car accident that would change my life. I was driving along enjoying the ride in my 1997 Toyota Corolla, when a woman ran a red light, hit the back quarter of my car sending me into a 180 degree spin. I was on an overpass when she hit me. There was another car, with an infant in the back seat that I ended up hitting in the back, thankfully not injuring the baby. As the impact occurred, I reached across the front seat of my car in an attempt to keep my passenger from getting injured. In doing so, I injured my arm. When the airbag deployed on impact, I sustained injuries to my chest and face. Once the movement stopped, I tried to get out of the car. I couldn't open the door, so I kicked the door open and in the process, injured my knee. I made the trip to the hospital in an ambulance; so did my passenger. Out of everyone involved in the accident, we were the only two people injured. Obviously, my little

Corolla was the other injured party. It was the first car I had ever owned on my own and had bought new only 6 months before.

When I was released from the hospital the next day, I went to look at my car. It looked like an accordion. I cried. I couldn't imagine how the people in it could have actually gotten out alive. It was most certainly totaled. The pride I felt owning my first new car was crushed just like the wreck of what was left.

Even though I had only spent a day in the hospital, the injuries were major. I was unable to walk without aid since my injured knee couldn't support my weight and the injuries to my arm, my chest, ribs and face caused immense pain. In addition, I was home alone with my children who I was raising on my own. My busy life came to a painful, screeching halt. My new daily routine consisted of physical therapy three times a week and caring for my early teenaged kids. I wasn't used to being alone during the day. I was bored out of my mind.

One day, during a conversation with a friend who owned a limo business, I realized that I had the skill set and the technical knowledge that could put the systems in place that he needed in order to manage his business effectively. I offered to help. I said, "Let me answer your phones. I'll come up with a schedule to create some type of management system for your cars and drivers, so that we can actually make it all work. You'll then be able to see where your cars are and if they are available for you to do something on the fly." One of his challenges was that there were other car and cab companies that would call him if there was an emergency or overbooking to hire his cars. Without a system, he didn't know whether he could facilitate them. So, from the comfort of my home, while I was recovering from my accident, I did what I do best. I got myself a computer, and I created a system that worked. I also created a website for him. I wasn't aware of it at the time, but at that moment, I had my very first client in what was soon to become my new business. Thank God for technology.

My limo-owning friend had a friend who owned a business. That business needed the same thing I had just set up for my friend; a system that allowed him to focus on his clients instead of worrying about all of the administrative stuff in the background which kept him from moving his business out of the stagnant standstill it was in. He couldn't handle it on his own; that's where I came into the picture.

As I was working with these clients, I had a revelation; "This is something that other people could do. I'm surprised that nobody else has really looked at doing this." So, I started researching online. I found out that, not only *were* other people doing this kind of work, there were actually Virtual Assistant Organizations. That's what I was doing, assisting people, virtually with their businesses. I joined a couple of those organizations and went through some of the courses they offered.

Then, in 2000, the doctors said "Okay, you can go back to work." .... Okay; what do I do now? I was used to the money and needed the money. My long-term disability was about to be cut off. Yes, I was enjoying what I was doing with my virtual assistant business, but I was still learning. I needed to go back to work. The firm I had worked with had spaced out my job because I was doing several different roles. I was also an AVP there; Associate Vice President in an administrative role. The management had changed while I was gone and they didn't have those titles anymore; there was no place for

Shift Your Beliefs to Get What You Want

me. Ultimately, the firm paid me three months' severance and said, "Go find another job."

I landed in the financial industry again, this time with a mergers and acquisitions firm. From the beginning, I let them know that I had a small business of my own on the side. I didn't want to give it up. They were fine with it, which was amazing to me, because I came in as their office manager as well. I worked with them for 3 years, still slowly growing my own business. Then, I caught a huge break when I got a client on the west coast. I was doing their marketing when social media first started really hitting high. That client introduced me to another client and then another. I wasn't even marketing my business, it was being referred.

I was living in Pennsylvania at the time and commuting into New York City to work every day; it was a 2-hour commute. I purchased a laptop and an internet air card so I could work on my business on the way to work and on the way home. Then, when I got home, I was working some more for my clients. I was basically doing my full-time job and growing my business on the side. I was living up to my business name.... Ambicionz! I did that for nearly 8 years.

One day, I was at a networking event and someone I was talking to asked me about my business. When I told them that I was working my business part time, they said that if I really wanted to see my dream of owning my own business come to fruition, I needed to look at my business as a full-time job, and my corporate job as a part-time job.

It wasn't the hours worked that made one job a full time and the other part time; it was how I perceived the 2 jobs. I began looking at Ambicionz as my one and only full time job. It was that shift in belief that set me up for success in my business. The nine to five was my "means to an end." The more I thought of it like that, the more my client base grew in Ambicionz.

It finally got to a point where I was too tired to do both. I was up until 1 o'clock in the morning, working on Ambicionz and waking up at 4 o'clock in the morning to get ready for the commute into the city again. I was working on my way into work and on my way home. There was that STRESS again. In 2008, I finally decided to let go of the "means to an end" so I could concentrate 100% on my business. That was a huge leap of faith for me. My business had been consistently growing and I knew it was the right decision.

Immediately, I started volunteering with the International Association of Virtual Assistants (IVAA) in several different areas. I totally enjoyed what I was doing and realized that I was getting great exposure in volunteering for them. I was being referred to people within the organization who needed help with programs that I knew well; and my reach back into the world from my home office began to grow within that organization.

Then, to my surprise, I got nominated to the board. The knowledge and expertise I had been sharing in the forums got me the nomination and I was elected to a three-year term. My first year was in the membership department, then I was approached to become Vice President. I had proven myself as a business owner, having longevity and a wide skill set. I was also consistently increasing my technical knowledge and what was happening in the industry. So, I was elected to Vice President then, in following the IVAA protocol, I was appointed the position of President.

Today, I create my own economy. I have found a sense of freedom, a sense of purpose and personal fulfillment in the work that I do. Not that there weren't some of those ingredients before, but now I am the one in control of my stress level, my time and my finances. It also allows me to use creativity that longed to be unleashed.

I have freedom in my life today that would not have been had that accident not happened; and there are wonderful people in my life who have supported me along the way.

I encourage you to trust that everything happens for a reason. Maybe it's happening to lead you to a place where you can follow your own Ambicionz!

About the Author

Doreen DeJesus retired in early 2009 after twenty-three years in Corporate America. Her extensive training includes office management, social media implementation and management, event coordination, author support, strategic online marketing, project management, multimedia presentations and much more. In order to provide her clients a diverse skill set, she has completed certification for the following: Social Marketing Specialist Internet Marketing Specialist, Master Shopping Cart Specialist, Professional Virtual Authors Assistant, Certified Travel Planner, Certified Real Estate Assistant, Graduate Virtual Assistant.

Doreen is proud to be an active and past member for many online and local organizations that support the Virtual Assistant Industry.

Additionally, Doreen is an active member of several mastermind groups which help promote and develop the skills of entrepreneurs.

Learn more about Doreen's **Ambicionz** at www.ambicionz.com or connect with her at ddejesus@ambicionz.com .

Shift Your Beliefs to Get What You Want

Collaboration: The Model That Works in the 21st Century

Paula Fellingham

To best address our growing social, political, and economic problems, I believe humanity needs to incorporate the Collaboration Model in the 21st Century, rather than continue with the age-old Dominance Model, if we are to move away from poverty and war and toward prosperity and peace.

The Collaboration Model has as its highest priority the caring for people. Its focus is the creation of mutually beneficial relationships.

Simply stated, the Dominance Model is about top-down control and the Collaboration Model is about creating healthy, sustainable relationships. The first is based on the need to dominate and control; the second is based on the ability to trust and collaborate.

Historically, humanity has been subjected most often to the Dominance Model. Why? Because power and riches usually go to those who dominate, whereas trusting collaborators are generally open, vulnerable, and risk being dominated by their partners.

Since the Dominance Model is top-down, like nation over nation, religion over religion, man over woman, examples including any relationship or system where domination occurs. Since domination has been a consistent theme throughout history, those of us living in the 21st Century can easily look back and agree that this model is not conducive to peace. On the contrary, the Dominance Model causes, rather than discourages, conflict and war.

I believe at this critical time in history the world needs more people who are willing to create collaborative relationships based on mutual respect and mutual benefit. Additionally, more equalitarian relationships (relationships based on equal rights) are needed today in our families, in our businesses, and in our governments. Those who understand and practice these models will surge forward successfully, and those who do not, will not.

As with most things that are beautifully simple, collaboration begins with our thoughts, our attitudes, and the questions we ask ourselves.

Those who think abundantly ask, "How can I help you?" and/or "How can we help each other?" before asking, "What's in it for me?" They who ask such questions have the best chance of succeeding with the Collaboration Model in their personal relationships and in their businesses.

People who genuinely desire to create mutually beneficial relationships authentically seek to create win-wins. The good news is that those who aren't naturally inclined to think abundantly can easily be taught to do so. It's a matter of wanting to learn a better way of being, then

Shift Your Beliefs to Get What You Want

acquiring the tools and practicing until old "dominance" thoughts, habits, and patterns are changed.

Succeeding with the superior Collaboration Model is about being "others-centered" rather than "self-centered." Others-centered leaders work to find ways to make life better for those in their circles of influence. Self-centered leaders work to find ways to make their own lives easier and better. Their genuine concern for the welfare of others is low or non-existent. Through the ages, benevolent leaders have been revered and dominant leaders have been feared.

One of the things I learned from my friend Riane Eisler, *Roadmap to a New Economics,* is that if we are to create new, more sustainable and equitable relationships and systems that have the power to dissolve anger, discontent, and inequality worldwide, we must discuss the roots of the problems. We must go deep into matters that statisticians, theorists, and conventional economic analyses often ignore. We must discuss basic values and human needs that are often minimized or ignored in the Domination Model that prevails, in varying degrees worldwide, across all "isms" of government (capitalism, socialism, and communism) and across all types of relationships and businesses.

A healthy, open discussion about values and human needs is prerequisite to moving the world from the prevailing Dominance Model to the superior, and much needed, Collaboration Model. Since we are co-creators of our problems, as co-inhabitants on this planet, it behooves us to discuss solutions together.

The first step to creating Global Collaboration might be cross-country discussions about how individuals and nations can collaborate for mutual benefit. We're talking about developing partnerships on a massive scale. Can this be

Conversations That Make a Difference

done? Absolutely! Why will it work? Because at the end of the day the Human Family does care about the same things: prosperity and peace.

So to all who believe that creating mutually beneficial relationships are superior to top-down control... to those who believe that caring for people should be a high priority for lawmakers, let's dialogue.

Let's begin by talking about which basic values and human needs should be part of a society based on the Collaboration Model.

Caring, by definition, suggests we consider all life as valuable. It follows, then, that the life of a child is far more valuable than stocks or bonds. And if we believe that our children and families are more valuable than financial instruments, our economic policies and practices should reflect that. Societies should insist on practices that encourage health and good education for all. Policies created should encourage such things as individual and national productivity; financial and economic sustainability.

Are not our values skewed when massive money is spent on warfare and rockets while masses of people are suffering because their basic needs are not met?

If we believe that the real wealth of the world lies in the contributions of humanity, then caring for people should be our highest priority. And laws that promote human development should be created at all levels of all governments as natural outgrowths of those beliefs.

If you believe in these principles then an appropriate question is, "What's next?" And a congruent action step is to gather with those who care deeply about the future and are willing to:

1. Create in-country roundtable discussions where

participants of varying social and economic status meet and discuss solutions within the context of the Collaboration Model.

2. Dialogue among nations at semi-annual conferences where every country is represented.

3. Create grassroots and government support for the Collaboration Model.

The obvious challenge with discussions that involve participants from different backgrounds and cultures is the problem of differing perspectives. Indeed, the gaps between the haves and have-nots, cultural differences, religious differences, etc. pose a threat to the success of the proposed roundtable discussions and international dialogues. However, if participants can agree on long-term goals such as prosperity and peace, healthy discussions about how to accomplish those goals can include the elements of collaboration.

Old thinking assumes that top-down control will inevitably continue, but history proves that model is broken. New thinking leads to partnerships and to policies that value people and their needs. And that model works. It's time for new thinking.

I believe that the individuals, families, businesses, and nations that adopt and adhere to the Collaboration Model will not only enjoy increased prosperity, they will help lift the level of love and peace on earth in powerful ways, never before witnessed in the history of the world.

I am sending out a CALL FOR ACTION.

Who am I to do this? I am one woman who leads one

organization: The Women's Information Network (The WIN) www.theWINonline.com. I know the hearts, the needs and the desires of the women of the world. They want prosperity and peace and they're willing to do almost anything to get it. Millions of women worldwide have been victims of the old Dominance Model.

Now is the time for new thinking, new action, new strategies that work. It's time for kindness, caring, and collaboration.

Shift Your Beliefs to Get What You Want

About the Author

Dr. Paula Fellingham holds a Doctorate of Education in Human Relations. She is the author of five books and numerous magazine articles.

Paula is the Founder and CEO of The Women's Information Network. www.theWINonline.com. (The WIN) The WIN helps women worldwide live their best lives. WIN eTV Show Hosts www.eTVforWomen.com are now presenting 1,000 Global Women's Summits in 176 countries.

Dr. Fellingham received the "Points of Light Award" from U.S. President Bush, and the "National Volunteer Service Award" from President Obama.

For over three decades Paula was a world-renowned speaker, and for years she hosted her own radio show, two hours daily.

Paula's family performed professionally as a musical group across the U.S. and in Europe for twelve summers.

Paula Fellingham's mission is to strengthen women and families worldwide. Paula has been married for forty-four years. She is the mother of eight children and twenty-three grandchildren.

Email: paula@theWINonline.com
Call: 866. GO WOMEN (866.469.6636)

Hey Problem, You're My Friend!

Dr. David Laughray

Life can be full of problems. Everyone knows that. To desire a problem-free life is foolish. *What problems mean to us is the only issue.*

First of all, know that problems are a sign that you are alive. Problems exist because you have commitments. I'll say it again, a little differently. Only people with commitments can have a problem. No commitments; no problems. Big commitments can lead to big problems. Think about it. Your problem exists because you have a commitment.

Problems point to what is missing. You notice what is missing because you want something. It is not there, and that becomes a problem. For example, money problems exist when you have a commitment to pay your bills and money to do that is missing. Relationship problems exist when you have a commitment to live happily with someone and harmony is missing. You have a health problem when you have a commitment to feel great and your energy is missing. A flat tire is a problem for someone needing to drive their car. But, it is not a problem for his or her three year old.

Shift Your Beliefs to Get What You Want

I trust you get the point. You will most likely never be free from problems. Knowing this can produce a breakthrough. You are free to live in a powerful way.

Most people do not live in power. They live in fear of problems. They become prisoners to their problems. They handle them in one or two ways: anger or confusion. Their conversation is, "This is not fair and I am really upset about this" or "I don't get it, I did all the right things." These people are stuck at the problem level. Their life is about trying to fix the problem. The problem becomes the issue because it represents loss. Nobody likes to lose. But, instead of focusing on how to win, they focus on how do I avoid losing? How not to get a problem? Instead of having the inner conversation "How do I get what I want?" they say, "How do I not get what I do not want?" Big difference, huh?

If you want to be free to create your life instead of reacting to events, there is a third approach to problems which gives you power. Problems become your friend

It all begins by using your *Moment of Power*. Your Moment of Power exists in the space between "what happened" and the interpretation or meaning you give to "what happened." You consciously stop your "knee jerk" reaction to a situation as bad or I don't want this. Instead you choose to replace it with another interpretation Instead of anger or confusion, you can say, **"This is my opportunity to wonder."**

The following Wonder Formula has produced many powerful breakthroughs for me and for many of my clients. It is my privilege to share it with you

W: What's in this from God? There are many beliefs about God and for the sake of this formula your particular definition doesn't matter. In general, most people believe that God is Love. **So, just ask the question, "What is in this from God?"** The truth is that at any given moment what is *bad* is always available and so is what is good. But, God is only Good. So look for what is good. Where is the God in this? What can I decide to love about this? A Law of Life to remember is *whatever gets your attention ends up getting you.* In your Moment of Power you **say to yourself, "I know only good can come from this."** Then ask, **"What is my commitment?"** Your commitment is always good. Focus on this, and go on to the "O."

O: Opportunity is all around me. We are always surrounded by countless opportunities to reach our goal. Many solutions are always available. Look for new doors to open and new opportunities. You can make new commitments. **Ask yourself, "What new possibilities exist for me?"** Let life show your new ways. Be open to the flow of newness waiting to come into your life.

N: Now is when I choose to act. You cannot solve today's problem by comparing it to the ones you had in the past. "Later" or "someday" will not take care of the problem. Ignoring it doesn't work either because (and here is another Law Of Life) *what you "bury" you "bury" alive.* NOW is the time to take action towards your commitment. Make your mind up to fully live in the now, because *tomorrow is today multiplied.* **So, say to yourself, "This is the most important moment of my life. This is the moment I can think a new thought, see a new possibility and take action on it."**

Shift Your Beliefs to Get What You Want

D: Drop my demands. All suffering comes from unmet expectations. You did not expect to have the problem, but you have one. So, stop demanding that it go away. Stop demanding that life look a certain way. You have every right to have positive expectancy, but expectation sets you up for failure. Your freedom and happiness does not depend on how life looks or what people do. **Repeat these words, *"I joyfully accept all the unacceptables in my life just the way they are."*** Let me be clear. This does not mean you want what is unacceptable, you just accept it. What good would it do not to?

E: *"Everything always works out."* Say this to yourself over and over again.. This means you have faith that your problem will be solved or won't even be an issue. Just keep moving in the direction of your commitment knowing that answers and results will unfold perfectly. They always have and always will. Isn't it true that many of the problems of the past were blessings in disguise?

R: Rejoice, no matter what. Remember to laugh. Joy produces clarity. Decide to make someone else laugh. Give your joy to others. When you give, you receive. **Say to yourself, *"Nothing can take away the joy at the center of my being. I gladly give joy to my world."*** Practice *advanced gratitude* by giving heartfelt thanks for the realization of your commitment. Rejoice in advance that everything you need to create your dream is moving into your life. See it, feel it, and celebrate!

There you have it: real conversations that make a difference

Conversations That Make a Difference

I have one more idea to share with you about the power of wonder. Every morning start your day this way. **Say out loud with enthusiasm the following:** *"I wonder what fantastic thing is going to happen to me today."*

You get what you expect!

About the Author

Rev. Dr. David Laughray has been devoted to helping individuals Awaken Their Greatness for over three decades. He has provided over 500,000 opportunities for people, nationally and internationally, to experience and access his leading edge life transforming ideas.

Holding both a Doctor of Divinity Degree and a PhD in Psychology prompted L.A. Times to call him, "*An American Original.*" Donald Trump refers to Dr. Laughray as "*The most memorable career coaching experience of my life.*" Deepak Chopra says Dr. Laughray will create "*much success in the field of infinite possibilities.*"

Dr. Laughray's Awaken Your Greatness Group works with Fortune 500, political and entertainment professionals through strategic alliances with Norm Freed PhD whose client roster includes: Tom Hanks, Sharon Stone, Tony Robbins, Secretary of State Colin Powell, Michael Eisner, DreamWorks, Vivendi, L'Oreal International, Xerox, and Hyatt Hotels International.

Dr. Laughray is the co-founder of Wakeup Spiritual Center.

DavidLaughray.com

WakeUpSpiritualCenter.org

A Note of Gratitude

Thank you so much for purchasing this book. It is the second in the *Conversations That Make a Difference* bestselling series. I'm sure many of these stories have touched your heart.

A number of the authors, who have openly shared their stories, want to offer you a gift. We invite you to visit our virtual gift suite at

www.wakeupwomenconversationsgifts.com

where you will be able to gain access to those gifts. Once inside the gift suite, you will find a description of those author's gifts and a link to take you to that author's page which was created for the express purpose of sharing their gifts with you. Choose as many as you would like, and ENJOY!

If you have not already read the first book in the series, we invite you to go to

www.conversationsthatmakeadifference.com

to get your copy of this best seller. It is available in Kindle and print.

We also invite you to keep visiting our page for updates on the next book which is already in progress.

Wake Up Women is committed to bringing you outstanding stories of inspiration and transformation that make a difference. If you have a story to tell please visit

www.wakeupwomen.com

and click on **Be a Contributing Author** to obtain information on how you can become an author in the *Conversations That Make a Difference* bestselling book series.

Gratefully,
Karen Mayfield
Founder of Wake Up Women